No More Bad Shots

No More Bad Shots

Shot by shot, round by round—
a foolproof guide to better golf

Hank Haney
WITH John Huggan

NEW YORK, NEW YORK TOTAL Sports Illustrated™ KINGSTON, NEW YORK

SPORTS ILLUSTRATED, and *Total*/SPORTS ILLUSTRATED are trademarks of Time Inc. Used under license.

For information about permission to reproduce selections from this book, please write to:

Permissions

Total Sports Publishing

100 Enterprise Drive

Kingston, NY 12401

www.totalsportspublishing.com

Cover design: Todd Radom

Interior design: Joseph Rutt

ISBN: 1-892129-97-3

   Library of Congress Catologing-in-Publication Data

Haney, Hank
  No more bad shots / by Hank Haney with John Huggan.
   p. cm.
  ISBN 1-892129-97-3
  1. Golf. Huggan, John. II. Title.

GV965 .H25 2001
796.352'3--dc21

                                                       00-054539

Printed in Canada

Acknowledgements

To all my students who have made teaching golf such a rewarding challenge for me over the years.

To my colleagues Tim Cusick and Steve Johnson for their help and friendship.

To my favorite writer from Scotland, John Huggan, and my long-time photographer, Dom Furore, for all your help.

To Randy Voorhees and John Monteleone of Mountain Lion, Inc., for giving me the opportunity to help more golfers.

To John Jacobs and Jim Hardy for giving me the knowledge to be good at what I do.

And always, most of all, to Mark O'Meara for being a special student.

To my wife,
Jerilynn,
for your never-ending support.

CONTENTS

Mark O' Meara works hard on his game.

Introduction

My motivation for writing this book was simple. As someone who spends his life working to help people of all shapes, sizes, genders, and golfing abilities play better golf, it occurred to me that every one of my pupils has at least one thing in common: They all hit, or believe that they hit, too many bad shots. That's why they come to me for lessons.

Of course, there's really no escaping that feeling. Not forever anyway. It's an unfortunate truism of the golfing life that we all hit bad shots now and again. In fact, let's be honest here. Every golfer who has ever lived hits more bad shots—or at least imperfect shots—then he or she hits good ones.

Years ago Ben Hogan, who labored through many unsuccessful seasons on the PGA Tour before finding a swing that worked for him, recognized that reality. Asked how many shots he was happy with in an average round, Hogan, who became perhaps the greatest ball-striker in the game, said that the answer was invariably no more than two and was more often than not less than that.

There are, of course, two ways of looking at such a daunting statistic. It is a clear indication of just how difficult this infuriating game can be for even the most talented individuals. On the other hand, the fact that the likes of Hogan struggle at times does give some hope to all of you out there trying to improve your game.

The same is true of the top players you see every week on your television screens. It may appear at times as if they are playing a "different game"—to an extent they are because their scores are so much lower—but these great players have more in common with you than you may think. Even Tiger Woods, who already has proved himself as the greatest golfer of all time, has hit his share of bad shots and has things he has to watch for in his peerless swing. The bottom line for all of us is that the game of golf is a constant and never-ending search for perfection, whether we're number one in the world or number one million.

Tiger Woods with his coach, Butch Harmon, working to make the best, better.

But there is always hope. Especially if you apply yourself to improve your own game and don't get too bogged down in the many and varied theories on how the golf club should be swung. Far better that you identify the problem areas and tendencies in your own game and then work to fix them, rather than toil away trying to produce some theoretical "ideal" golf swing.

The best way to identify your route to improvement is to first identify your bad shots. Start with your driver. It is the longest club in the bag and has the least loft, so any sidespin imparted on the ball by the clubhead will be exaggerated by the straightness of the face. More loft on the clubface produces more backspin on the shot and so less sidespin. That's why we all find it easier to hit the ball straight with a 9-iron than we do with, say, a 3-iron.

There are only two ball-flight possibilities when it comes to the curvature tendencies your shots can have—three if you include a straight shot, but I'm assuming you don't want to fix that one! Depending on the characteristics of your swing, you are either going to be a hooker or a slicer of the golf ball. Generally speaking, if your club swings on too upright a plane and not enough around your body, you will tend to slice the ball—the ball curving from left-to-right in the air. If your club swings around your body on too flat a plane, you will be more inclined to hook the ball—the ball curving this time from right-to-left in the air. If your club swings on the correct swing plane for you (and there is no one correct swing plane for everyone, but everyone does have one swing plane), you will have the best chance of hitting a straight shot. There is no guarantee, of course. Your

Hitting shots with your driver—the straightest-faced club in your bag—will tell you a lot about your shape of shot. *Above Left:* Mark O'Meara. *Above Right:* Sergio Garcia. *Below Left:* Jesper Parnevik. *Below Right:* Mark Brooks.

An overly upright swing tends to lead to a slice shot, the ball curving from left-to-right in the air.

An overly flat swing tends to lead to a hooked shot, the ball curving from right-to-left in the air.

swing still needs to be timed correctly, but you will maximize your chances of success if your swing plane is correct.

There are plenty of other possibilities to consider when analyzing someone's ball-flight. Players who tend to slice the ball—the vast majority of golfers—also tend to hit the ball too high. They might also be inclined to hit the ball fat with their irons and tend to "sky" shots hit with their driver because of the relative steepness of their actions. On the other side of that particular equation, players

who tend to hook the ball will generally have trouble getting the ball into the air. They tend to hit the ground behind the ball, which leaves them prone to both fat or thin shots, albeit those of a different variety to the slicer. But more of all that later.

I also see a lot of other bad shots during my hours giving lessons on the practice range. There are many possibilities why these bad shots occur, but the reasons remain the same. For example, the upright swinger is more likely to hit the ball off the toe of the club;

shots hit off the heel of the clubface tend to be struck more by those whose swings are on the flat side. With the club coming into the ball on an improper plane, it is hard to find the center of the clubface on a consistent basis. So, yet again, the shape of your swing dictates to an enormous extent the type and quality of the shots you will hit. This fact remains true for the short game. The steeper your swing is, the more prone you will be to hitting fat pitch shots; the club contacting the ground before striking the ball. Equally, the flatter your swing, the more you will have a tendency to "blade" pitch shots due to the relative shallowness of your downswing plane. Either way, you simply have trouble hitting both the right amount of ground and the ground in the right place as you strike the ball. (No doubt, by now some of these shots will be disturbingly familiar to you!)

All of which, in fact, leads to the biggest problem I see when it comes to short shots. It isn't hitting the ball the correct distance. It isn't creating the right amount of spin on the ball. No. It is simply getting the ball into the air on a consistent trajectory. These impact or ball-flight mistakes are caused by swings that are either too upright or too flat.

Of course, pitching the ball into the air should always be something of a last resort for all golfers. It is far easier to judge distance and control the flight of the ball if you hit your shots around the green as low as you possibly can. In other words, putt whenever you can. If you can't putt; chip. And only if you can't chip should you consider lofting the

Around the greens, keep the ball as low to the ground as you possibly can. Chip only when you can't putt. Pitch only when you can't chip.

ball skyward. Golf is a hard enough game without introducing unnecessary complications. Keep things simple. Always hit the ball as low as possible, given the situation you find yourself in.

This same principle holds true once you are on the green. In my experience putting problems stem mostly from an excess of movement—whether it be from the body or from the hands and arms—during the stroke. People seem unduly keen to see the result of their efforts and so introduce an extra moving

If you're like most people with putting problems, you have too much body movement in your stroke.

part into what should be a simple back and through motion of the clubhead.

The good news is that this book will help you identify and, more importantly, help you eliminate the bad shots from your "repertoire." You'll still hit bad shots, of course. We're all human and these shots never really completely go away. But the quality of your bad shots can certainly be improved. If, all of a sudden, your worst effort is finishing on the edge of the fairway or green instead of ten

yards into the rough or in a greenside bunker, your scores are sure to start tumbling. It may sound curious, but the key to better scoring is better bad shots.

The frequency and severity of your bad shots is what largely dictates your level of play and the number of strokes you take to negotiate 18 holes of golf. Your good shots are less significant. Not only—as we have already said—are there fewer of them, most player's good shots are approximately the same in quality. Bad shots, on the other hand, cover a much wider range. That is why their elimination, or at least their reduction, is so important.

Think about it. Let's say you play off an 18-handicap. That means you are supposed to—on at least a typical par-72 course— make a bogey on every hole. But, if you are like most 18-handicappers I have encountered, you don't play that way. Consistency isn't exactly your strong point. You may shoot the 90 your handicap says you should, but it is achieved with, say, a few pars, a few bogeys, and two or three disaster holes. Not 18 straight one over par holes.

My point is this: Those disaster holes stem from the hitting of at least one really bad shot, sometimes two—topping, duffing, a slice out of bounds, skied tee-shots, shanking, thinning. . . . The list is endless and isn't pretty reading. These bad shots play an extremely important role in determining your eventual score. That's why you need to get rid of them. Read on.

Why You Play

At this stage, ask yourself a question. Don't worry, it's an easy one. Or maybe it isn't; maybe you've never really thought about it before. If you haven't, think about it now.

Why do you play golf?

Consider your answer carefully. Your response is important and will influence which parts of this book will be most useful to you on the road to having more fun with the game.

More specifically, ask yourself what you get from playing golf. We are all different and we all play for our own individual reasons.

Do you play simply for the exercise? Nothing wrong with that, of course. Studies show that walking three or four miles a couple of times a week is good for your over-all fitness.

Or is there, for you, more to it than just enjoying the fresh air?

Do you play for the competition? Does beating your friends on a Saturday morning fulfill the competitive side of your personality? Again, that's fine. We have all felt the satisfaction that comes with a hard-fought victory on the last green. It's a nice sensation, one that helps make golf the great game that it is.

Or is golf, for you, more of an inner challenge? Do you play golf because you want to improve your swing? That's a noble cause. And never ending. I have yet to see anyone, not even my star pupil, former Masters and

Many people play golf simply for the exercise. Walking a few miles each day has obvious health benefits.

British Open champion Mark O'Meara, make a perfect golf swing.

Or is golf, for you, simply a matter of shooting the lowest score you can? That's hard to argue with, too. The aim of the game is to get the ball into the hole in the fewest number of strokes.

Or is golf, for you, a less complicated affair? Is all you want from the game the thrill that comes from hitting the ball a long way? I have no problem with that either. In fact, such an ambition makes you in the

Respect between opponents—as shown here by Tiger
Woods and Jack Nicklaus—is one of the most
enjoyable aspects of golf. A good, hard-fought match
is a lot of fun.

majority, if the practice habits I see from the people at my driving ranges are anything to go by. I don't see many bodies out there on the putting and pitching greens; the vast majority of my pupils are instead beating balls with their drivers and long irons.

In the end, however, why you play golf doesn't really matter. There is one common factor in all of us: we all compete on the course or hit balls or take walks with clubs in our hands for one reason—golf is FUN.

Twenty-five years as a teacher has shown me that fun is what everyone is looking for in golf. At the end of the day it has to be that way. If something isn't fun, why do it at all?

So, take it from me, no matter what part of the game is fun for you, that little word is the single reason why you are playing this often infuriating but always fulfilling game. The bottom line is we all play golf for fun.

Fun

Okay, we've identified the need for enjoyment as the reason you play golf and, of course, are reading this book. Which is just as well, because this book is designed to get you to enjoy your game more, whatever your motivation for playing may be.

Let's take a closer look at just why you play golf. The challenge of the game is fun for people. Indeed, that is why most people play golf. It is, after all, a game; something to do with your recreation time.

The thing that I see at my facilities is that people like to hit the ball, and they like to hit it well. That's number one on most people's wish lists. Like I've already said, it isn't the short game.

That is why I am often puzzled when I go to seminars and listen to teaching pros say that pupils just don't work enough on their pitching, chipping, and putting.

Why should they? Who are we as teachers to tell people what they should be doing to have fun? If fun for you is hitting the driver a long way and straight, then that's what I would always encourage you to work toward.

The first thing I always ask one of my teachers after he or she has given a lesson is, "Did your student have fun?" Then I ask if that pupil hit the ball better. That's where the fun is for most people. Some may equate their level of fun with the number of shots they have taken to play all 18 holes. For those people, the fastest way to lower scores is to improve their short games, the shots hit from within 100 yards of the hole. But these players are in the minority. In my experience, most of you simply want to hit the ball better and longer.

Now, that may seem surprising to you. Especially when, as we are all agreed, the ultimate point of the game is to get the ball in the hole with the fewest strokes possible. But think about it. Hitting the ball better and longer is going to help you achieve just that goal. I've asked some of the dedicated ball-beaters I see every week why they work so hard on their long games. They believe that if they can hit the ball better more often, then the score will take care of itself. And

Above: John Daly is one of the biggest draws to the game—all because of the enormous distances he hits the ball. Length is sexy.

Right: Jose Maria Olazabal possesses one of the best short games in golf. Few are better at turning three shots into two around the greens.

that, I have to say, is a point of view I have a lot of time for.

When I see students whose scores don't match their abilities to swing the golf club or strike the golf ball solidly, I tell them to spend some time around the pitching green and on the practice green. I tell them to go work on their short games. If you have a really sound swing and the numbers on your cards don't reflect that fact, then the problem has to be in your work on and around the greens, or your ability to manage both

yourself and your game on the golf course.

Of course, that's one of the funny things about golf. Your ability to score well isn't necessarily what provokes admiration among your peers. In golf, a kind of inverse snobbery exists.

Here's how it works. Someone who hits the ball well—and a long way—is always going to draw a larger crowd than the guy who gets the ball up and down for par all day long. That's just a fact of life. Why do you think more people rush to watch John

Daly than, say, Jose Maria Olazabal? Olazabal may be the better player—he's certainly the better scorer day-to-day—but that isn't what most people want to see. No. They want to be able to hit the ball as far as "Long John." In golf, distance is sexy; chipping and putting isn't.

So your ball-striking is much more likely to cause people to stand back and admire your game. In the minds of most golfers you're not playing golf properly unless you are hitting the ball solidly, up in the air, and making it go a long way.

In contrast, guys—such as Olazabal—who get the ball 'round the course in a decent score largely by virtue of their ability to scramble and turn three shots into two, only gain a grudging respect most of the time. To the majority of spectators, that isn't "real" golf.

Having said that, there is nothing wrong with wanting to improve your ability to score, but you have to understand that such a process doesn't involve you getting out on the range with just your driver. Not often anyway. Instead, you'll have to spend most of your practice time around the chipping and putting greens.

In my experience, that isn't what the vast majority of my pupils want to practice. They don't want to hit grounders all the way 'round the course and then chip and putt to make a halfway decent score. Why? That isn't much fun after a while. Everyone wants to be known as at least a reasonable ball-striker.

The Four Stages of Ball-Striking

In my lessons, I focus mainly on helping people correct their bad shots. To get students feeling like they are on their way to improvement, the first thing I do is change what the golf ball is doing in the air and, in particular, eliminate any recurring bad shots.

Hitting the ball is what most people focus on. It's what they enjoy the most, and it's the first of what I call the four stages of ball-striking.

They are:

1. Hitting the ball; making solid contact.
2. Hitting the ball in the air, on the correct trajectory.
3. Hitting the ball straight, or at least at your target.
4. Hitting the ball far; making it go.

So, only after completing all four stages of ball-striking do you really reach the point where you can learn how to actually play the game. I mean really play the game, which is why this book is organized the way it is.

Those stages of improvement and development never change. Whether you are coming to me for lessons as a complete beginner or as a low-handicapper, there is no difference.

That's another thing to realize about golf. Your career as a golfer isn't going to be one long upward curve. More times than not, improvement through change will be preceded by a—hopefully short—period of misery and suffering as the alterations made to your technique have a chance to properly kick in. While I do expect you to improve the day after you read this book, keep in mind that it may not happen in the first five minutes out on the range! In all likelihood, you will hit a few bad shots before you get a proper sense of the new feel and moves you are practicing. The fact is that golf is a very difficult game. It is never easy, and changing your swing habits will always be a challenge.

Because it only takes a second or so to swing the club and hit the ball, your life on the links is always going to be all about error correction. Golf isn't a—"Do this, this, and this, then this will automatically happen"—kind of game. You just can't possibly think about too many things in so short a time.

That is why, if you are like most golfers, you are confused about what you should be thinking about on the course. How can you be otherwise? If you are not clear as to what you are doing wrong, how can you possibly know what it is you should be working on or thinking about before, during, and after each shot?

The answer is in your golf ball. What you should think about depends on what your ball is doing and what your club does to make the ball do something wrong.

So when people ask me what they should be thinking about at address, or on the take-away, or on the back swing, or on the down-swing, I can never say for sure, not without watching them hit some shots. Any advice I give depends on what their mistakes happen to be. Those mistakes I am most concerned with relate to their ball-flight and their impact conditions when the club strikes the ball. That was the first thing I learned when I first began to teach golf. The great golf instructor from England, John Jacobs, taught me that valuable lesson. John is the best I have ever seen at fixing ball-flight, which is the essence of teaching golf.

When I teach I narrow that process down to how each individual should feel and think at the various stages of the swing. Every one of us is different. We all start out with a certain swing and certain habits. So you need to know what to think about, what you should look like, and what you should feel—given your starting point.

So you ask, "What is the problem?"— instead of, "What are we going to do to fix it?"

Fixing Your Problems

More times than not, when you try to fix your golf swing, you should try to work in the opposite direction. If, for example, you are troubled by a slice, you should spend some time working a hook into your golf swing.

Sam Snead, one of the greatest players and swingers of a club in the history of the game, used that principle on his own swing. If Sam was having trouble with a slice, he wouldn't try to fix it on the course. Instead, he'd play as best he could with the left-to-right ball-flight he had on that particular day; then, after his round, he'd go to the range and try to hook the ball—the opposite shot of what he had been doing on the course.

There is no one swing thought for every golfer, although every golfer should have a swing thought. Bruce Lietzke *(left)* and Vijay Singh *(right)*, for example, have very different actions and, no doubt, very different swing keys.

Make that your approach, too. Recognize your mistakes, then try to correct them by doing the opposite. Search for the middle ground. The words and pictures on the following pages will help you get there. The focus of this book is that there are invariably three ways to do most everything in golf. For example, you either hit the ball straight, to the right, or to the left. There are no other possibilities.

But there are a lot more examples:

- You either hit the ball on the correct trajectory, too high, or too low.

- Your ball either flies straight, curves to the right, or curves to the left.

- Your grip is either neutral, strong, or weak.

- Your swing is either on-plane, too upright, or too flat.

- You either aim straight, to the right, or to the left.

The list is almost endless, but whatever the shot, there are nearly three ways to play it.

More times than not, you need to feel like you are doing the opposite. Feel is a much misunderstood thing. Particularly in golf. Think of it this way. If you're like most people you are resistant to change in almost every aspect of your life. It's natural to fight it. We all get comfortable over time. But in golf, comfortable is often the last thing you want to feel. Especially if you are making a change to, say, your grip. If the change doesn't feel funny, weird, or uncomfortable, chances are you need to make an even bigger change.

Let's say you are trying to weaken your grip by turning your hands to the left on the club. You'll need to do it more than you think. As a teacher I often have pupils who need to change some aspect of their game by at least a foot (to use that as a measure). But I find I'm begging for them to achieve just even an inch of change. It's that difficult to alter any aspect of one's game or swing.

So exaggeration is the thing. The tough part is that any change feels strange and awkward at first, so your inclination is to always go back to what is comfortable and familiar. But let me repeat: If something doesn't feel awkward or strange, you probably aren't changing enough. If you want to be better, your swing has to be different. And in order to be different, you have to feel different. The only way to get that different feeling is to exaggerate something that is pretty much the opposite of what you are currently doing.

Tips, Tips, Tips

Having said that, this book gives you a series of tips to help you get from where you are now to where you want to be with your golf game.

All these tips do, however, come with a warning. Take care with them. Be selective. Some will work for you; some may not. Watch out that you don't overdo something. Everything in golf can be overcooked. So when you start to see, say, your long-established and long-hated slice turning into a regular hook, you have gone too far. Retreat and search again for the middle ground.

On the upside, there are always different routes to take to achieve the same end. For each problem identified in these pages, there is more than one tip offered.

Besides, if you are like nearly every golfer I have ever met, you enjoy tips. Isn't there nothing better than the feeling of anticipation you get from working on something that may just be "the secret" for you? Exactly. Another great thing about tips is they are quick and easy to try. That's important. If you are like most golfers you don't have the time to practice as much as you would like, so time is valuable. Most people like instant gratification when it comes to the quality of their shots. And *everyone* is looking for the "secret."

Working on your swing on the range—as Tom Kite is
doing here—in the hope that you will find the "secret"
is one of the most enjoyable aspects of golf.

Research conducted by many golf magazines shows that quick, easy-to-try tips are among the most popular articles in their publications. Shortening attention spans are part of that trend, for sure, but there is more to it. You read these tips and then you go out on the course willing to try them in the hope that you will hit the ball better. You don't want to hear that you need to go away and work on this or that for six months and then, hopefully, you'll be better at golf. That's not enough for you. You want it all and you want it NOW.

I know this, and that's why I have filled this book with quick and easy things you can think about and apply to your own game. Some or all of these tips will help you right away. I guarantee it.

Don't panic if something doesn't work for you. If progress is slow, you need to:

1. Exaggerate any changes more than you already are doing;

2. Try another tip; or

3. Add another tip or two to go along with the one you are working on.

Let's say you are a slicer, your shots starting left and finishing right. It's not an easy fault to fix. Identifying the root of the problem isn't easy, for one thing. There are a number of different ways to hit a slice. So you may need to try a few of my anti-slicing tips before you hit on the right one for you. Be patient—but only for a while—with each tip.

Try them all, though. You might find that more than one tip helps you. You might also find that only one tip is for you. Or you might find that they all help straighten out your shots. The key to success is to have an open mind. If your attitude is as open as a slicer's clubface, you'll do just fine. I have total confidence in you as a student.

So what am I asking of you as you start to read this book? Not much. All you need to do is recognize and identify your bad shots. Watch what happens to your ball when you hit a bad shot. Pay attention to where your ball starts and how much and in what direction it curves with each of your clubs. Analyze your impact. Look at how deep your divots are. Where do they point? You need some of this knowledge if you are to going to improve, and these factors give you the essential information on the path, plane, and direction of your swing.

As well as the tips, this book is also a book of swing thoughts. Every player has some swing thought that they take with them on the course. Even the best players in the world go to the range before a round looking for the thought they are going to use during an upcoming round. Feel, like the weather, changes day to day. It is always amazing how the thought that worked yesterday doesn't often produce the same shots today or tomorrow. Like I said, golf is a constant search. It never ends, even when you think you have this infernal game licked once and for all!

Besides, a tip is really nothing more than a swing thought or the description of a feeling you should have to try and work toward something better. In this book, I will help you analyze what your thoughts need to be, then give you some examples of thoughts that will help you fix some of the mistakes you commonly make. But, be clear, this book is not simply a series of tips. There is some how-to information in here as well. You need this as a starting point if you are to find yourself and your swing in these pages.

If you apply all the fundamentals, then work in the right direction, before too long you will be a pretty solid golfer. Actually, you have to believe in that fact. You have to be positive in the midst of any sort of change to your method. Never forget that golf might just be the most difficult game you can play. Be patient with yourself. And make sure the process is fun.

Remember, too, that better golf is, as this book shows, all about the elimination of error. If you can get rid of at least one bad shot, it has to be worth the effort. Take my word for it, you'll be a more content, more confident, and more informed golfer as a result. And I'll be one happy teacher.

One last thing before we get started in earnest. Let me tell you the same thing I tell all my students. I've never failed to help anyone who has come to me for a lesson. And you aren't going to be the first. Stay patient and good luck.

Hitting the ball solidly is high on any golfer's priority list—from novices to top professionals such as Vijay Singh.

1

Hitting the Ball

For every golfer, from beginner to touring professional, making solid contact with the ball is essential to consistent ball-striking and shot-making. So, in a way, hitting the ball is not only the first stage of golf, it is a constant source of concern to every level of player. No matter how good you get at this game, how solidly you are hitting the ball is always going to be one of your first thoughts on the practice tee and on the course.

That said, when anyone comes to golf for the first time, his or her primary concern is making good contact with the ball. I can tell someone is a beginner by counting how often he or she misses the ball. That stage of wondering and hoping to hit the ball soon passes, however. Once regular contact is made between club and ball, the next step is to try to hit the little ball before you hit the big ball (the ground). Then it is trying to hit both at pretty much the same time. (You are also, of course, trying to hit the ball somewhere on the clubface and, later, off the sweet spot on a consistent basis.) Then it is

trying to hit the ball far. Then it is trying to hit the ball straight. Then it is controlling the trajectory of your shots as you would like. Do all of the above on a consistent basis and you can fairly call yourself a golfer. A good golfer at that.

But we are getting ahead of ourselves. Let's get back to basics.

There are five possible ways to make contact between the club and the ball. It doesn't matter what kind of player you are, what your handicap is, or what kind of swing you have—that there only five ways you can hit the ball is one of golf's immutable laws.

1. You can hit a shot "fat"—the club contacting the ground behind the ball and usually too high on the clubface.

2. You can hit a shot "thin"—the club coming in too far off the ground as it contacts the ball, which is struck too low on the clubface.

3. You can hit a shot off the toe of the clubface.

4. You can hit a shot off the heel of the club-face.

5. You can also hit the ball off the middle of the clubface. And that, of course, is the one shot you want to produce time after time.

What influences each of these five shots are the keys to you beginning to understand your own swing and then working to improve it.

Let's start by defining each shot. The first step toward improvement is to understand where your problems lie.

Fat Shots—Swing too Steep, Divot too Deep

A fat shot occurs when the club swings down on too steep a plane, then digs too deeply into the ground behind the ball. It is one of the worst shots in golf. Not only will the ball generally finish only a few yards somewhere in front of you, hitting the ground behind the ball also tends to jar your body. Your wrists will hurt. And your hands. And your elbows. And your shoulders. The green-keeper isn't going to be too happy with you either, seeing those big deep holes in his golf course.

It's a common bad shot, though. Take a look at any driving range in the world. Hardly any grass, right? The reason for that is simple. Most golfers tend to swing too steeply down into the ground and, as a conse-quence, dig too deeply with their clubs.

Some of this is due to the mistaken notion that to make the ball go up you have to hit

A fat shot—the club contacting the ground behind the ball—typically occurs when the club swings down too steeply from the top of the swing.

down—only one of the many clichés that serve only to confuse golfers. And some of the come down to what you might call the "hit" impulse—hitting at the ball, rather than swinging through it.

Look at it this way. Most golfers slice. That's a fact. Most golfers don't use their hands very well through impact. That's another fact. The result of either or both is

Swinging to the left in an effort to avoid a slice and to stop the ball finishing to the right only causes the ball to curve more from left-to-right.

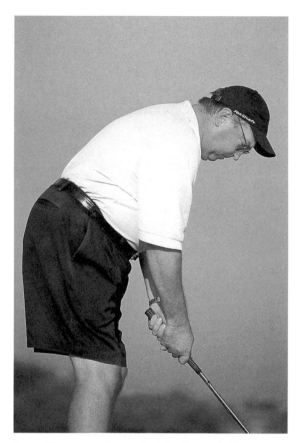

One of the worst pieces of advice in golf is "keep your head down."

that a lot of people swing the golf club to the left in a vain attempt to compensate for a left-to-right ball-flight. I say "vain" because, although swinging to the left does at least get the ball started to the left of the target, it still has to slice back if the shot is to finish "straight." Plus, the more you aim left, the more you will slice. So the original fault only gets worse. It feeds on itself. More to my point—a swing moving to the left tends to be steeper than it should be. So the club digs more. So the slice gets worse. So the divots get deeper. So the grass continues to disappear. So our friend the greenkeeper gets more and more upset.

Other factors contribute to an overly steep swing. Most people, when they are introduced to golf, are told to "keep their heads down."

Bad thought.

Understandably, many beginners overdo what they assume is sound advice. They setup to the ball with their chins almost stuck to their chests and their eyes glued to the ground. When they try to swing the club back away from their ball, their ability to do so freely is restricted by the rigidity of their head position. In other words, the left shoulder, instead of turning under the chin, merely "bounces" off it. The only way to avoid that, of course, is by tilting your shoulders, which is exactly what golfers who keep their heads down too much tend to do.

Keeping your head down too far at address prevents you from making a proper turn behind the ball and automatically sends the club "up" more than "around" on the backswing. You are, in effect, too much over the ball at what passes for the top of the backswing and so are condemned to make an overly steep downswing. The end result? The club strikes the ground behind the ball, loses most of its momentum, and sends the shot only a fraction of the distance required.

Instead, think of it this way. On the backswing, your shoulders turn at 90 degrees to your spine angle. Your arms should swing the club up and around in one motion. Both are equally important. You need some of each— the around and the up and down—one must not dominate the other. Too much "up" or too much "around" will knock the club off plane and sooner or later lead to steepness in your swing. In other words, if your left shoulder goes down and under and your right

On the backswing, your shoulders should turn 90 degrees to the spine angle you created at address— just as Steve Elkington has done here.

shoulder goes up too much on your backswing, the shaft of the club will be too steep and you will almost inevitably "stick the club in the ground."

And there's more. Even with a sound setup and a good shoulder turn it is still possible to swing the club on too steep of an angle. Here's how. Your arms could lift the club too much on the backswing or you could take the club back too much to the inside on the takeaway, which forces you to swing down too steeply. Either one can make the club dig into the ground too much. Indeed, that fatal steepness can be introduced at any point in

Tilting your shoulders on the backswing—left shoulder too low, right shoulder too high—puts the shaft of your club in too upright a position.

the swing. Your job is to locate where you have a problem, then fix it accordingly.

Where to Look for Your Problem

Okay, we've covered the symptoms and results of fat shots, but if you're like every other golfer on the planet, you're more interested in the causes and cures. So it's time to

identify yourself, or at least your swing tendencies, in the following descriptions.

As I said in the introduction, you must first know your problem before we can find a cure.

As with so many things in the golf swing, potential problems can start at address. And that is certainly true of fat shots. The wrong position before you start makes it difficult at best for you to make a decent swing.

Good posture is a relatively exact science, but not completely so. At address you should be bent forward about 20 degrees from your hips. Your knees should be slightly bent. Your head should be up off your chest. Your back should be close to straight. That's all you need to know—and copy.

Fat shots are most often caused by a tilting rather than a turning of your shoulders during the swing. The first thing to check is your posture at address. If you are bent over more from your hips than you should be, your shoulders will have a tendency to rock as the club moves back and through.

Fat shots can, however, also happen if your posture at address is good. At least they can if you don't turn your shoulders level enough. A bad shoulder turn is still possible from a good setup.

A good setup does give you a much better chance of making a good turn during your swing. A bad setup virtually condemns you to failure before you even start. If you bend over too much, you are always going to tilt your shoulders too much, unless you stand up just the right amount in your backswing.

At address you should be bent forward about 20 degrees from your hips. Your knees should be slightly bent. Your head should be up and off your chest. Your back should be close to straight. Again, Steve Elkington is close to perfect.

Bending over too much at address almost inevitably leads to you tilting your shoulders on the backswing.

That's tough to do on a consistent basis and just one more compensation you don't need in your swing. The bottom line? The golf swing is a chain reaction. Getting it off to a good start is the easiest route to a good shot.

The best thing to know about proper posture is that anyone can do it correctly. You don't need great athletic ability to be able to stand to the ball in an athletic position. There is no rhythm or timing involved. By definition, your setup is just a position and therefore relatively easy to reproduce or copy.

Having said all that, there are two specific kinds of fat shots—steep fat and shallow fat. The results are similar; the causes a little different.

A deep divot mark is one symptom of a "steep fat" shot.

Bad Shot: Steep Fat # 1

If this is a shot you are plagued with, typically your divots will be on the deep side. If you are removing large quantities of turf—especially with your irons—you need to flatten out your swing.

Focus first on your hands and arms. Try to get them to swing more around your body rather than up and down in a straight line. Practice with the club held up, maybe a foot off the ground, then gradually work your way down until the clubhead is sitting on the turf. This will give you the feel of a flatter hands-and-arms swing. Then try to reproduce that feel with the club on the ground. Hit some shots, too, off a sidehill lie with the ball above your feet. The slope of the ground will force you to swing flatter. Feel how your forearms rotate away from the ball, then back on the through swing.

Bad Shot: Steep Fat # 2

Another cause of steep fat shots is too steep of a shoulder turn. In other words, you are tilting rather than turning.

Stand as if at address with your arms across your chest; right hand on left shoulder, left hand on right shoulder. Now turn trying to keep your shoulders as level as possible. Keep your left shoulder up as much as possible. Don't let it dip.

As with most of these exercises, chances are you won't do it enough at first. So exaggerate the opposite feel. It's a feel, not reality.

Bad Shot: Shallow Fat # 3

This is a case of too flat a swing that leaves the club too far behind the hands and arms on the downswing. I see this bad shot more in

To level out your turn both back and through, practice swinging with the club raised off the ground. Gradually lower the clubhead while trying to repeat the feel of the previous swing.

Right: Hitting shots off a sidehill lie—the ball above your feet—is one way to encourage the feel of a less upright swing.

  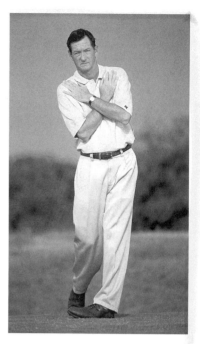

Flatten your shoulder turn with this exercise. From "address" try to turn your shoulders as level as possible, both back and through.

A "shallow fat" shot can result from you leaving the clubhead too far behind your hands and arms on the downswing.

After emphasizing the rotation of your left arm as the club moves back from the ball, feel as if your arms are dropping and your left arm is rotating back down and into your side on the downswing.

Thin Shots—Swing too Shallow; Little or No Divot

A thin shot is the opposite of a fat shot, although those who tend to hit the ball thin can often be prone to the odd fat one, too. That happens when the club "drop-kicks" into the ball. If the plane of your downswing is too shallow, the clubhead bottoms out behind the ball and skids into impact, catching the ball thin.

More commonly, however, too flat a plane to your downswing causes the club to barely hit the ground—or even miss it altogether—with the result of the ball hitting near the bottom of the clubface. That's "thin." The upside is that thin shots tend to fly fairly straight. The downside is that they typically fly too low, and they are also hard to control in terms of distance.

Where to Look for Your Problem

The thin shot is on the other end of the scale from a fat shot, so any faults are, generally speaking, the opposite of those you see in players prone to fat shots.

Thin shots can stem from a posture that is too upright—your body too straight up and down. From this position, you tend to turn your shoulders too level, which in turn makes it difficult for you to swing the club down into the ball on the proper angle. In this case, that approach is too shallow; the swing bottoms out too far back and the club skids into impact or the bottom of the swing is too far forward, which leads to a thin contact between club and ball.

Feel the club swinging down in front of your body coming into the ball. This will give you the correct angle of approach to hit solid shots.

good players who are perhaps fighting a hook by dropping the club to the inside on the way down.

Here you need to emphasize the rotation of your left arm as the club moves back from the ball. Then, from the top, feel as if your arms are dropping and your left arm is rotating back down and into your side. As you'll see, this is a similar fix for a hook.

Thin shots can result from an overly upright posture at address.

Some players create an overly upright posture by lifting up at some point during the swing.

Just as with fat shots, of course, this overly upright posture can be introduced once the swing starts. I see many players "standing up" as they swing the club back from the ball.

Then again, a sound posture and a good turn on the backswing are no guarantees of solid contact. It is also possible to swing your arms too flat, thus putting the club on that shallow plane that invariably leads to a thin shot. Or you could simply drop the club to the inside on the way down. Or you could get close to impact, but then fail to turn your body through the shot. Or you could rise up out of your correct posture on the downswing. As with steepness, shallowness can be introduced to a swing at *any point*. Your job is to locate where in your action the problem occurs.

Bad Shot: Topping

I think it's safe to say we all agree on this next point: topped shots are perhaps the ugliest in golf, second only maybe to the shank . . . and just as destructive.

There's just no getting away from the fact that topping a shot is also embarrassing. You have, after all, almost missed the ball, the club just making contact with the very top of it . . . sometimes just its top coat of paint.

That said, there are three different types of tops. They all look the same in that the ball doesn't go very far or very high, but they have distinct characteristics. Let's look at each in turn.

Bad Shot: Mis-radius Top

The most common cause of this shot is the simple loss of posture during the swing. What typically leads to this is a swing that is too steep and destined to smash into the ground. Instinctively feeling this will happen, leads you to lift up during the swing in an attempt to make room between yourself and the ground.

This move, of course, changes the distance between every part of your upper body and the ball, which is disastrous unless you have extending arms. As you lift up and pull back, your arms cannot reach the bottom of the ball. So contact is made halfway up or higher, with the result being a topped ball.

Focus, yet again, on your posture. Get it right at address. Rid yourself of the steep swing plane during your swing just as if you were fixing a steep fat shot. Then try to main-

Maintaining your posture throughout the swing is one way of fixing a tendency to hit "mis-radius" topped shots. Justin Leonard is a great example to copy.

tain your posture throughout your swing. Key in on your rear end. A lifting of the upper body during the swing is really a loss of the forward bend in your hips. So keeping your rear end "out" as you swing will maintain the angles you set up at address.

Bad Shot: Steep Top

This is an especially ugly member of the topping family. It results from a very steep downswing, the club coming almost straight down on top of the ball from the outside. The resulting shot is invariably a "grounder" to the left; the ball coming off the bottom of the club or the heel.

Before all that happens, however, the player usually takes the club away too much on the inside, lifts it to the top, and then comes over the ball on the way down.

If that sounds like you, try making some practice swings while trying to develop the opposite loop. Feel the club swing more underneath on your backswing and down from the inside at the start of the downswing, then more up and to the right as you swing through to your finish.

This shot is also a close relation to the slice, in terms of the swing that produces it. So work through the slicing check list that follows later in chapter three.

A steep top results from the club coming almost straight down into the ball from the outside. The ball typically trundles off low and left. Not a good combination!

To get rid of the "steep top," swing the club more out on the backswing, then in on the downswing. It should feel as if your downswing is "underneath" your backswing.

A "shallow top" shot stems from the club approaching the ball on too flat a plane.

Bad Shot: Shallow Top

As you'd imagine, this shot is the exact oppo-site of a steep top, although the end result is somewhat similar. The only real difference is that this time the ball usually skitters off to the right rather than the left.

This shot is caused when the club approaches the ball on too flat a plane and, usually, too much from the inside. To put it another way, the club is already close to the ground when it is still well behind the ball. When that happens, solid contact is unlikely at best. The causes are familiar to you by now—an arm swing that is too flat; a shoul-der turn that is too level; or dropping the club in behind you from the top.

Work on correcting all three causes by focusing on making a steeper arm swing and shoulder turn on the backswing, then com-plete a better rotation of your left forearm down and into your body just after you change direction.

These corrections will get the club more out in front of you and help you approach the ball on the correct angle. Do them and you'll soon be hitting solid shots.

Toed Shots

A ball flying off the toe of the club can have any number of possible ball-flights. It depends on all the other factors—swing plane, clubface angle, direction of swing—that can con-tribute to your impact conditions. Generally, however, a toed shot results from a steep swing, the ball curving to the right.

There are other possibilities. A shot may come off the toe because the clubface is very closed and the toe gets to the ball first.

To combat a tendency to hit "shallow tops," work on rotating your left forearm down and into your side as the club starts down from the top of the swing.

But, if you tend to hit off the toe end of the club and take deep divots, your shots will curve to the right. If you tend to hit thin shots off the toe, you'll hit more hooks. Whatever your tendency, shots hit off the toe will always be harder to control and will fly shorter than normal.

Where to Look for Your Problem

If your body is turning too slowly—knocking your timing off—and you hit behind the ball and tend to hit a hook, then the toe of the club is getting to the ball too quickly.

If, however, you hit the ball pretty straight, not curving your shots to the right or the left, but still make contact off the toe, then the solution may be a simple one. It might just be your distance from the ball, either at address or during the swing. In other words, at some point you are either

If you hit a lot of shots off the toe, you may be standing too far from the ball—either at address, or because you have pulled back at some point in your swing.

Heeled Shots

A shot flying off the heel of the club tends to be a slight fade; starting left and finishing right. It also tends to end up pretty straight, so it usually won't get you into too much trouble. That's the upside. The downside is they don't fly very far, they don't look very pretty, and you're not going to have a lot of fun hitting too many of them. But at least with the wooden clubs they are good misses. Not with the irons, though. Get too close to the hosel and you will be hitting shanks— perhaps golf's most destructive shot and one we will be fixing later.

If you have a tendency to hook the ball, you could be hitting off the heel because your swing is too flat. Maybe this stems from your posture. Maybe it's your turn, or your arm swing. Maybe you are dropping the club in too much behind you from the top.

Then again, a heeled shot can also result from a slice swing. When you swing from the outside or to the left, that brings the heel of the club to the ball before the toe.

Where to Look for Your Problem

Again, the root of your problem can often be simple to find. If you are hitting the ball pretty straight and you are hitting the right amount of ground, yet your shots are still struck on the heel of the club, you could be out of position at address and standing too close to the ball.

Let the shape of your shots tell you where to look for the problem.

standing too far from the ball, or moving back onto your heels away from the ball during your swing.

Ideally, your arms should hang down directly beneath your shoulders. Assuming you have a good posture and your weight is even on your feet from heel to toe, then that condition should be easy to reproduce.

Shanking often stems from a tendency to swing too much to the inside early on the backswing.

Work on making your backswing more upright by placing a bag to the right of your ball, then swing back without the club touching the bag.

Bad Shot: Shanking — Heeled Iron Shots

For those of you afflicted with what can be a terrible disease, the shank shot is a painful subject. Sending the ball off at a 45-degree angle isn't a whole lot of fun and, left unchecked, this shot can lead to people give up golf entirely. Before you take that drastic step, there are some things you can try to rid yourself of what is certainly the most destructive shot in the game.

A shank happens when you swing the club too much out in front of you, the hosel connecting with the ball, which sails off to the right at the aforementioned angle.

The problem, of course, could be a simple one. You may just be standing too close to the ball. If that is the case, stand back a little, give yourself more room to allow the center of the clubface to hit the ball.

Then again, you may be swinging the club

Cure your shanks by hitting shots without touching a head cover on the ground just outside the ball.

A friend holding your head will help you eliminate your falling forward "into" the ball during the swing.

Reaching out too much with your arms is one way to hit a shank.

Keeping your upper arms close to your sides, like Tommy Armour III does here, will stop you from reaching out too much on your downswing.

too much to the inside on the backswing. That puts the club too far behind you, and, later, too far from your body as you swing through.

What you need to do is swing the club more up and down with your hands and arms. In other words, keep the club more in front of you going back.

After you have worked on that move for a while, test yourself. Lay a head cover on the ground just outside the ball, then try to hit a short pitch shot without the club touching anything but the ball and the ground. If you aren't hitting the head cover, you know the club isn't too far in front of you.

There are also two other ways you can shank. Although you might be set up the

correct distance from the ball, it is possible for you to get too close as you swing. In other words, you could be "leaning in." To combat that move, you need to focus on keeping your head back, away from the ball. A friend can help with this by resting his or her hand on your head as you swing, resisting any forward movement from you.

Alternatively, you might just be reaching out with your arms as you swing the club through the ball. That will put the clubhead too far from you and, more disastrously, lead to the hosel of the club contacting the ball. If that sounds like your problem, the good news is that it is easily fixed. Simply concentrate on keeping your upper arms close to your sides as you swing down and through.

How high or low you hit the ball is largely due to two factors: how fast you can swing the club, and the amount of loft on the clubface at the moment of impact.

2

Too High, Too Low, and How Far?

So far, every bad shot we have looked at has been linked to club-ball contact. Now it is time to move on. There is a natural progression here. Bad shots are not just the results of poor contact between club and ball. Sometimes you can hit the ball right out of the middle of the face and still see a poor result.

I'm talking, of course, about shots that fly okay, but that sail off to the right or to the left of your target. Or they fly too low. Or too high. In other words, the problem is not hitting the ball, but producing the correct flight or trajectory.

The trajectory of a shot is determined, to an extent, by where the ball contacts on the clubface. For example, if the club hits the ball low on the face, the shot will fly lower than if the ball came off the middle of the clubface on the sweet spot.

That makes sense, but there are other factors why balls fly to targets. Indeed, the biggest influences on the trajectory of your shots are the clubhead speed your swing generates and, of course, the amount of loft on the club at impact.

The faster you swing the clubhead, the more spin you put on the ball, so the higher it will tend to fly. If you swing at 80 MPH, you aren't going to hit a 5-iron as high or as far as someone who swings that club at 100 MPH. That's just a fact of golfing life.

So, everyone has his own trajectory, but there is no one trajectory for everyone. And the correct trajectory for you is determined by how fast you can swing the club.

If you are unhappy with the trajectory of your shots, there are a few places you can look for a solution.

Start with your equipment. If you aren't physically capable of producing a lot of clubhead speed—or at least not as much as you would like—you need clubs that have more loft and a lower center of gravity. That's why

I always recommend that someone with a relatively slow swing carry lofted fairway woods rather than long irons.

On the other hand, if you are capable of swinging the club at well over 100 MPH, you don't need that sort of help. Which is why you don't see many tour professionals—who generally produce swing speeds well into three figures—carrying 5, 6 and 7-woods. They don't need that extra loft; they can get by with only one fairway wood, usually a 3-wood.

For example, Tiger Woods carries only a 3-wood. But he has a 1-iron in his bag. Annika Sörenstam has nothing longer than a 5-iron in her bag, but carries four or five lofted woods. Those club set decisions are determined to a great extent by the speeds of the player's swing, although the particular course the golfer plays on a given week can also be a factor.

Too High, Too Low

Let's talk first about a tee-shot. Placing the ball on a tee can have a big influence on how high you hit your shots.

When you use your driver, I recommend you tee the ball so that half of it is visible above the head of the club at address. You want to hit the ball when the clubhead is level to the ground or even slightly on the up swing. This gives your shots maximum power and keeps the ball from flying off the top of the clubhead.

With an iron, the effect of a tee on the trajectory of the shot is lessened. Because you

If your swing is relatively slow, carry more lofted fairway woods than long irons. They will help you hit longer—and higher—shots.

want more of a downward hit through impact, the ball must be teed lower than it is for a driver. Make that *a lot lower*. Teeing the ball too high is one way to produce a weak shot with a higher trajectory than you would want.

Ball position has an influence here, too. Where you should place the ball within your stance varies for each club. For the longest

At address, about half of the ball should be visible above the head of your driver.

With your irons, tee the ball a lot lower than you would with your woods.

club—your driver—the ball should be opposite your left heel. As the clubs get shorter, move the ball back towards the center of your stance. But no more than that. For your shortest club, the ball should still, if anything, be slightly ahead of center. You don't want too much downward motion, even with a wedge in your hands.

The more you put the ball forward in your stance the more you add loft to the club. As the ball moves forward, your hands are, in effect, moving back. If your hands are behind the ball at impact you will hit a higher than normal shot.

Equally, the more you put the ball back in your stance, the more you de-loft the club. As the ball moves back, so your hands move forward. Reproduce that at impact and you will hit a lower shot.

Above: When hitting a driver the ball should be opposite your left heel at address.

Left: For wedge shots the ball should be opposite the middle of your stance.

Moving the ball forward in your stance effectively adds loft to your club and helps you hit the shot higher. Doing the opposite "de-lofts" the club and leads to a lower shot.

In more general terms, if your shots are flying too low, you are simply not getting to the bottom of the ball.

There isn't much we can do about the speed you swing the club, so focus instead on getting the right loft on the club and the right angle of approach into the ball. Anytime you are hitting down, you are de-lofting the club; any time you are hitting up, you are adding loft. Anytime you are level, you have neutral loft on the club.

In other words, if you have the right angle of approach—not up or down too much—and your trajectory is either too high or too low, the loft on your club is wrong at impact. At some point in your swing you are either adding or subtracting loft from the club.

So check where it is off. Is it at the top of the swing? If the clubface is open at the top, you'll have a tendency to hit the ball too high; if the clubface is closed, you'll tend to hit the ball lower.

The clubface could be closed or open because of your grip or your wrist position. Paul Azinger has it shut at the top of his swing and hits the ball low. He also has a very strong grip on the club with his hands turned well to the right, which leads to a closed clubface (looking skyward) at the top. You can see that same closed clubface in a golfer whose left wrist is bowed at the top of the swing. That changes the loft on the club and is the reason why Paul hits the ball lower than most players.

On the other side of the ledger, a higher than desired ball-flight can be the result of a weak grip, where your hands are turned too much to the left on the club, or an open wrist position at the top of the swing. Both would lead to an open clubface position (the toe of the club pointing down to the ground at the top). The open clubface is a characteristic of Fred Couples' swing. Fred's left wrist is "cupped" or bent back. Note, however, that such is his talent and speed, he is quick

This is the most common mistake that women make when they first start—bowed left wrist at the top (the clubface looking skyward), which produces a very low shot.

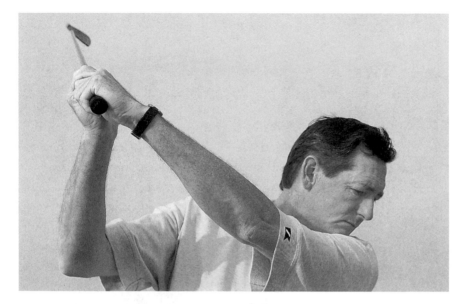

A neutral top of the swing position sees the left wrist flat and the clubface angled at 45 degrees.

An "open" clubface position at the top of his swing (the toe of the clubhead hanging straight down) is a characteristic of Fred Couples' action.

enough to square the clubface at impact. But, in most golfers, if that cupped left wrist position was maintained through impact, considerable loft would be added to the club, causing a higher and weaker shot.

The ideal or neutral top of the backswing position happens when the back of your left wrist is flat and the clubface is angled at 45 degrees, between the open and shut positions I have already described. Whatever side of that fence you are currently on, work on moving the top of your backswing position closer to neutral. Do that and you will soon be hitting the ball on a more appropriate trajectory for your clubhead speed.

As for your downswing, the more your upper body stays back in a reverse-C position the more you will add loft. However, the more you turn through—your right side moving through the shot—the more you will tend to de-loft the club. Justin Leonard does

that and hits lower than average shots as a result.

Whatever side you are coming from, try again to get back to the middle ground in terms of your body motion and the releasing motion of your hands and arms. The release should feel as if you are rotating—counter-clockwise—your forearms and the back of your left hand through impact. You should have the sensation of leading the clubhead with the back of your left hand. There should be no adding or subtracting of loft from the club. Do this correctly and your shots will be straighter and more powerful—and on the proper trajectory.

Left: Turning his right side aggressively through the shot means that Justin Leonard hits lower than average shots.

"Scooping" with your hands through impact can add loft to the club and your shot.

Above: To hit shots on the correct trajectory, feel as if you are leading the clubhead through impact with the back of your left hand. Your hand is, in effect, a mirror image of the clubface.

Distance

One of the great things about golf is that just about anyone can hit a shot almost as well as the best players in the world . . . at least in terms of the quality of the strike. But that's as far as it goes. One thing you and I can't do is hit a drive as far as Tiger Woods does.

I believe that the minimum amount of clubhead speed needed for a driver in order for a pro to play on the PGA Tour is 110–112 MPH. You need at least that to be competitive. Anything more than that is a plus. Tiger is, at worst, a "triple-plus" relative to most of his competition. His everyday swing speed is somewhere around 135 MPH, and the scary thing is he has a lot more in his tank if he needs or wants it.

Now, I'm sure you already knew that without me telling you. Fair enough, I hear you say. But I'm equally sure that, like every golfer I have ever met, you would like your drives to be longer.

Distance has that effect on people. Distance is sexy, even if, in golf, direction is at least as important. However, distance, to a much greater extent than your accuracy, dictates your potential. For example, you need to at least hit the ball far enough to get to all of the par-4s in two. If you can't, your scores are only going to be so low. Nobody's short game is so good that they can get up and down in two *every time* for par.

Again, that's obvious. But what you may not have realized is that pure distance helps your accuracy. I bet you've heard that more distance means less accuracy. Maybe. But it also gives you more accuracy with the clubs

The fact that Tiger Woods can hit a mid- to long iron as far as most people can hit their drivers is a huge competitive advantage.

you hit for your approach shots. In my world, a 7-iron goes straighter than a 5-iron, and a 5-iron goes straighter than a 3-iron. And so on.

If you hit two or three clubs less into a green, you are going to hit the ball straighter just because of the physics of it. The more you hit under the ball, the more backspin you produce . . . and backspin fights sidespin. When you look at players who hit the ball a long way, you often see how wild their shots are. Well, they wouldn't be hitting it wild if they were holding back. If you hit the ball 230 yards with your driver, Tiger Woods is only going to need a 4-iron to get out there that far. He could hit every fairway with that club. He can hit his 4-iron straighter more often than you can with your driver. So distance, in a sense, gives you more accuracy.

Still, if you're like most people, you could use more distance. It would lower your scores and increase your enjoyment of the game. If you ask one hundred people if they would rather take two less putts per round or hit the ball 10 yards farther, at least ninety of them would go for the increase in distance.

Even 10 yards makes a big difference. And it's fun. Plus, it's an ego thing. Like it or not, all golfers are judged, at least partly, by how far they hit the ball.

Where You are Losing Distance

If you're like most people you're not swinging the golf club as fast as you could. You're not using your maximum speed. A lot of the reason for this is the perception that you should swing the club smoothly and slowly. You look at pros and think he or she swings the club so smoothly yet hits the ball so far. But those two things—slow swing and hit far—don't really go together.

Players who hit the ball a long way have a lot of clubhead speed. It might not look as if they are swinging the club hard, but they are swinging fast. Most people don't use all the power they have in terms of the fact that *they could swing faster.*

How to Find 20 More Yards

Want 20 more yards? First, take a wider stance. This will automatically give you a

A wider stance is the first step towards longer shots.

wider arc. The wider your arc, the more you can produce clubhead speed. Don't get tense, though. The softer your arms are and the looser you are at address, then the faster you can move your muscles.

Also, when you set up you don't want too much weight on your left side or your right side set too high. That would put you in position to hit down too much. You want to hit the back of the ball. It's vital that your angle of approach sweeps the ball off the tee.

Your grip is important, too. A grip that is turned more to the right—stronger—will help you hit the ball longer, because it will close the clubface, and a closed clubface produces longer shots that tend to hook the ball. A closed stance helps as well. Pull your right foot back, then turn it out more than your left foot. This gives you more turn on the backswing and gets the club more on the inside, which should help you draw the ball.

Keep your arms soft at address. Tension leads to a loss of distance.

Fred Couples, a long hitter, is a great example of a relaxed and fast swing.

Set up with most of your weight on your right side, your right side a little lower than your left side.

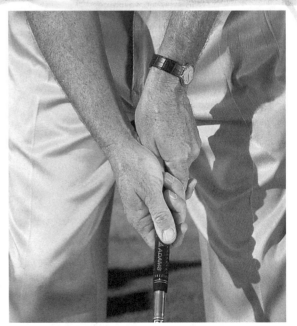

A stronger grip—both hands turned to the right on the club—will help you hit the ball farther.

A closed stance—your right foot drawn back from the ball-target line—will help you make a bigger turn on the backswing.

At the top of your swing, it should feel as if your back faces the target.

More Turn?

The answer to that question is a definite maybe. If you are as flexible as Tiger Woods, resisting with your lower body and turning with your upper body would give you more coil and, in turn, more clubhead speed. But most people have a hard enough time making a decent-sized turn, so don't worry about resisting with your lower body. Far better to let it go.

Instead, feel like your left shoulder is turning behind the ball so that your back is facing the target at the top of your backswing. There should be a feeling of stretching on the left side of your back as if you have turned all the way around and behind it.

Now you are in position to swing the club into the back of the ball as hard as you can. If you have X amount of clubhead speed and apply it directly into the back of the ball you will hit it longer than if you were hitting down or up too much. Either is a waste. You want all your force directed into the back of the golf ball in order to maximize your clubhead speed.

Delaying the release of your wrist cock allows you to create more clubhead speed through impact. *(Left)* Steve Elkington. *(Right)* John Cook.

Save Your Hit

The more you delay the uncocking of your wrists coming into the ball, the more clubhead speed you will have at the ball. The feeling you want is one of you accelerating through the shot to try and limit how much the clubhead slows at impact. Yes, that will happen. It has to. It's the law of physics. As the clubhead hits the ball it has to slow down.

So, even if you have new technology on your side, the feeling you want to have is that you are delaying the release of your wrists as long as possible and that you are squaring the back of your left hand as you hit the ball.

Many golfers release the club too early on the downswing and their hit is all but spent before they get to impact. Delay your release and you will increase your clubhead speed at the ball—which is where you want it.

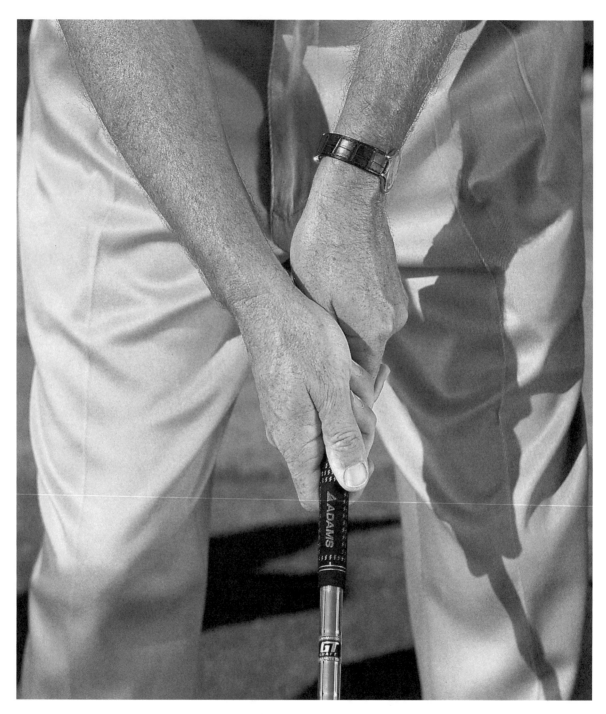

In a neutral grip, the back of your left hand and the palm of your right hand face the target.

3

Curing Your Curves

Everybody who plays golf has a tendency to curve the ball one way or the other. You may think you hit it straight, but you'll still have a tendency to curve it either to the right or to the left. You might call it a draw or a fade but it is still basically a slice or a hook.

If you aren't sure which way your ball would have a greater chance of curving, of if you aren't willing to admit to favoring a hook or a slice, here is a surefire way to find your ball-flight tendencies. Imagine you have a large tree in front of your ball. You could hit past the tree on either side. Which side would you choose?

If you feel more comfortable hitting a left-to-right shot, then a fade is your tendency or preference. If you are happier going with a right-to-left shaped shot, then your tendency will be to draw the ball.

You'll tend to see more of a curvature with your driver. It is the straightest-faced club in your bag, so it will impart the least amount of backspin on the ball. That fact alone makes

shots struck with your driver more susceptible to sidespin. So you see more curve with the driver than you do with any other club in your bag.

You're not going to curve your shots as much with your short irons. They hit more underneath the ball. When you do that you create more backspin. And backspin counteracts sidespin.

That said, let's assume you are bothered by too much curvature with your shots. Either too much left-to-right—a slice—or too much right-to-left—a hook. Here's where to look for the root of your problem:

A. In Your Grip

First look at the way your hands fit together on the club. If you have a neutral grip—the back of your left hand and the palm of your right hand facing the target—and a neutral swing, all other things being equal, you should hit a straight shot.

If you have a strong grip, where your

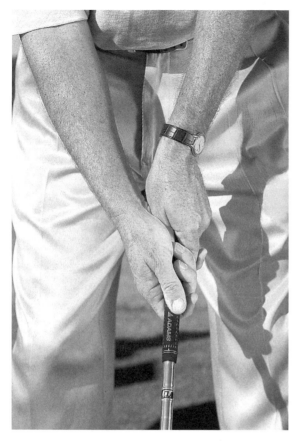

A strong grip means that your hands are both turned too far to the right on the handle of the club.

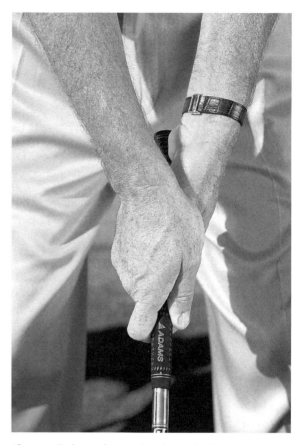

If your grip is weak, your hands are both turned too far to the left on the handle of the club.

hands are turned to the right on the club, you will have a tendency to hook the ball, unless you have a compensation built into your swing to block the face open at impact.

If you have a weak grip, your hands turned to the left on the club, you will tend to slice the ball. Unless, again, your swing compensates for your hold on the club and somehow squares the clubface at impact.

Take note, also, of your grip pressure.

Hold your club tighter if you want to get rid of a hook. A firmer grip will help elimi-

nate any excess hand action and slow down the squaring of the clubface at impact.

If you are fighting a slice, lighten your grip to encourage more hand action, which in turn will square the clubface at impact.

B. In Your Clubface Alignment

Clubface alignment at address can be a little confusing. Let me explain.

Those players who set up to a shot with the clubface closed (aligned to the left), usually

If you set up with the clubface closed at address, you will likely hit a left-to-right shot.

An open clubface at address tends to be a prelude to a right-to-left shot.

hit fades. That makes sense. Without an opening of the clubface at some time during the swing, the ball would fly where the face is aimed at address—straight to the left of the ultimate target.

The same is true for those players who address the ball with the face of the club open. They tend to hit draws because at some point in their swing they close the clubface in order to prevent the ball from flying to the right of the target.

In either case, the counteracting compen-

sation can also come at address. In fact, when you see players with an open clubface at address, they usually have a strong grip; their hands turned under the club. The opposite is also true. Players who set up with a closed clubface are likely to have a weak grip; their hands more on top of the club.

That's the thing about compensations. You always have to have an even number, with one canceling out another. The real problems start when you have an odd number!

Someone who hooks the ball is likely to set up with their left shoulder too high and their right elbow too close to their side.

Slicers set up with their right shoulders too high.

C. In Your Body Alignment

There are also body alignment characteristics to look for, depending on the shape of your shots.

If you favor—or fight—a hook you are likely to setup with your right side low and your right elbow tucked closely into your side. Your shoulders will also probably be closed (aligned to the right).

On the other hand, if you are more prone to a slice, you'll likely set up more "on top" of the ball, your shoulders open (aligned to the left) and your right shoulder higher than your buddies who hook.

As always, you can help rid yourself of either shot by squaring up your alignment.

D. In Your Stance

While your stance is important, the alignment of your feet is perhaps not quite as vital as you might imagine. Certainly, plenty of good golf has been played with both open and closed stances.

Be aware, however, that your slice could be at least partially a product of your open stance (your left foot pulled back excessively from the target line). Turning your left foot out too far—combined with a square right foot—can also encourage excessive hip turn and, for that matter, excessive shoulder turn through impact, causing a more left-to-right shot.

The same is true if you tend to hook the ball. A closed stance—your right foot toed out and back from the target line—will promote more turn in your backswing and less in your through swing. Less body turn through the ball means more hand action and more of a right-to-left shot.

E. In Your Turn

How you turn your shoulders has a big effect on the shots you hit.

If you tend to tilt your shoulders on the backswing and through swing—what I call a "rock and a block"—you will more times than not hit a slice, because the steepness of your shoulder turn will likely leave the clubface open at impact.

To combat that effect, focus on making more of a shoulder turn or even a little bit more of a hip turn on the backswing. This will help you make more of a rounded swing, cause less resistance in your lower body, and make it easier for you to hit the ball from the inside, thus squaring the clubface.

If you already fight a hook, focus on resisting more in your lower body as the club swings back. This will restrict your turn and, later, help your lower body turn faster to get out of the way as the club swings through the ball. All of which will help you fade the ball.

F. In Your Arm Swing

Just as tilting your shoulders produces a slice, so can an arm swing that is too much up and down.

Therefore it follows that an arm swing that is less upright—it should feel like you are swinging around your body—will give you more of a hook swing. The result of an arm swing that is too upright is, once again, a blocking motion with your hands and arms

To combat "rocking and blocking," focus on making more turn behind the ball on the backswing.

If you hook the ball, resist more with your lower body on the backswing, turn your hips no more than 45 degrees.

Swing your arms more around your body to combat a slice.

If your swing is too upright, you will always tend to "block" the shot with your hands and arms at impact.

coming into the ball. In addition, that upright arm swing will tend to put the shaft of your club in a "laid off" position. The more the club points to the left—that's laid off—the more you will tend to slice. Signs to look for are a left arm that is too high and rotated too much and a right elbow that is tucked in too close to your side.

If that sounds like you, try to point the club "across the line" at the top. The more the club is across the line (pointed to the right of the target), the more you will tend to hook the ball.

Focus on your right hand, arm, and elbow.

To hit a hook you want to feel like your right arm and elbow are up more at the top and that your right hand is tweaking the club to the right.

If, however, you are already across the line at the top and hitting hooks, you need to feel the opposite. You want to get the club to feel more laid off at the top of your swing.

Check the position of your arms. In all likelihood your right forearms will have rotated "under"—your right arm too much on top of your left with your right elbow "flying." All of which throws the club across the line.

To fight these problems, you need to lift your arms out in front of you on the backswing as you feel more lifting of your left arm and more rotation of your left forearm. And keep your right elbow down. That certainly will help your forearm rotation.

G. In Your Wrist Position at the Top

Another symptom of a hook or slice swing is the position of your left wrist at the top of the backswing.

A "cupped" wrist position (the wrist bent back) opens the face of your club and, barring a compensation on the way down, a sliced shot. Think of it this way: The more your hands are underneath the shaft, the more you will tend to put the clubface in an open position. Or, as your left arm goes in, your right arm lifts up.

A "bowed" wrist position (the wrist bent forward) does the opposite; it closes the clubface. The feeling that your left arm is up and your right arm is down will put your wrist in a bowed position. Or, your right arm is pulling in as your left arm lifts up.

Instead of these options, you want your left wrist in a neutral position at the top. In other words, flat. It's that simple.

H. Starting Down

Even if you make it all the way to the top of the backswing in a square position, things can still go wrong.

"Cupping" your left wrist at the top leads to an open clubface.

A "bowed" left wrist at the top closes the clubface.

A neutral left wrist keeps your clubface square.

The club should come down on the plane (a line parallel but above the original shaft angle). If it doesn't the club is either too steep—the shaft coming straight down into the ground causing a slice; or behind you (laid off)—the shaft too close to horizontal, which leads to a hook.

If you get the shaft too level, your right arm will lay down and your palm will face too much to the sky. In that respect, your right palm is a great reference. Feel as if it is facing ahead of you more to get the club back on plane.

The start of the downswing is vital, both in terms of rhythm and position. If, for example, your left arm rotates down into your body too much, that will steepen your swing and tend to make you slice.

If that sounds like you, feel as if you are laying the club off coming down. Also, feel as if you are getting your right palm to face up to the sky as you start the club down. This will reroute the club to a flatter position.

Ideally, your downswing should be on plane.

I. At Impact

The back of your left hand is key here. If you slice the ball, you are "hitting" with the side of your left hand. Straight shots are hit with the *back* of your left hand. If you hook, both hands have turned over too much. You always want to feel like you are hitting with the back of your left hand.

Make that your swing thought.

J. In Your Follow Through

On the follow through, the more your body hangs back and the more your lower body stops turning through, the more your hands are going to keep going, closing the clubface. That's going to lead to a hook, folks.

The more your body turns through—as fast as possible with everything moving through together—the more you will delay the closing of the clubface. So you'll eliminate your hook and, if your body outraces the club, you will hit a slice or a push.

"Hit" the ball with the back of your left hand.

Finishing in this position where your hips are turned completely through, will help get rid of your hook. Additionally, you can use the shaft of your club as a reference. If you finish with the shaft close to horizontal—more of a block finish—you will be holding the clubface open. That will cause a slice. To get rid of your slice, you need to release the club more. Let the clubhead go past your hands, the shaft ending pointing toward the ground. This is more a hook finish.

Slicing

The most common bad shot in golf is the slice. I would estimate that around 90 percent of all right-handed golfers hit the ball in the air from left-to-right. The opposite fault—a hook, the ball moving from right-to-left—is more commonly found in better players.

So, for the simple reason that it is the bad shot fought by most golfers, I will start this section of the book by covering in depth the slice and all of its many causes. It is, as we will see, a close relative of the fat and thin shots in that the steep swing seen in both is also a common characteristic of most slicers.

Bad Shot: The Slice

"Why do I slice so much?"

If I had a dollar for every time I have heard that question at the start of each lesson I would be a very wealthy man. If we can classify slicing as a golfing "disease," this affliction has reached epidemic proportions.

If the clubshaft is close to horizontal at the finish, you have held the clubface open.

There is no one cure for slicers. And just to make matters worse than they already are, there is more than one way to slice and more than one mistake that can lead to a slice.

Your slice can stem from your grip.

Ask any beginning golfer to take hold of a club for the first time and their natural grip will be with their hands in a "weak" position. That is, their hands are turned too far to the right on the grip.

This happens almost every time. If I tell a new pupil to let his or her arms hang down

If the clubshaft is pointing toward the ground at the finish, you have made more of a hook swing.

become more in vogue over the last decade and a half, but the hands still play a vital role in anyone's method.

Think about it. In all sports, athletes are judged to a great extent by the way they use their hands and feet. In some sports both assume equal importance, but in golf your hands have more to do than your feet. Which stands to reason. They are your only contact with the golf club. No other part of your body touches the club, so you can bet they play a big role in your swing.

Of course, a weak grip isn't the only source of a slice. Your slice can also stem from simple geometry. Let my explain. Because the golf ball sits on the ground below the level of the hands, there is a natural instinctive reaction to hit down on it from above. (Even if you have a classically orthodox hold on the club.) Hit the ball like that too much and your swing will get on too steep a plane, which in turn will produce a reverse rotation of your arms through impact. That opens the

and hold onto the club, the vast majority will hold it in a weak way. Nobody grips it strong—the hands turned too far to the left—by accident. And a weak grip makes it harder for you to square your hands at impact, which squares the clubface and produces a straight-flying shot. Most people's hands are not fast enough or active enough to square the club unless they have a strong grip.

Never underestimate the role of the hands in the swing. The "body" swing may have

As the only part of your body in contact with the club, your hands play an important role in your swing.

clubface, or at least makes it much harder for you to turn your hands naturally through impact in order to square the clubface.

Then again, your slice can be a product of your practice environment. Unless you are lucky enough to be a member of a club where practice facilities are a particular priority, you, like most people, learn or practice in conditions that are hardly conducive to the encouragement of a more rotary or rounded swing.

This is because you are hitting balls on practice ranges where there is little grass. A ball sitting on a bare patch of ground has to be "squeezed" off the turf. That sort of lie requires you to make a steep swing . . . if you want to make solid contact with the ball and get it into the air, that is. And, as I have already pointed out, that is one of every golfer's main priorities when hitting a shot. If the ball is sitting on bare ground, you have to hit down at least a little to strike the ball solidly. You have to get the club under the ball somehow. Trouble is, that downward hit also encourages a slice.

Be aware also, that slices, like so many other bad shots, are insidious beasts. A slice feeds on itself. The progression goes something like this: Player hits slice; ball finishes right of target. So player aims more left to compensate. So slice gets bigger. So ball finishes further right of target. So player swings more to the left in a futile attempt to compensate. So slice gets bigger still. And so on.

Hitting down too much can provoke a reverse rotation of your hands through impact . . . and a slice.

The Root Cause

It's misconception time and again. If you're like most people you think you slice because you swing "across" the ball from out-to-in through impact. Or you come "over the top" on the downswing. Or you fall back to your right side on the downswing. Or any number of other "causes."

Wrong, wrong, and wrong again. Those mistakes certainly aggravate a slice and make it worse, but they don't cause a slice.

A slice is caused by one thing and one

thing only—an open clubface at impact. Everything else is mere window dressing, a symptom of your slice rather than the root cause.

It's obvious if you think about it. The only way you can cut across the golf ball is with an open clubface. You can swing across all you want, but you will never hit a slice until the clubface is open. If the clubface is square with your out-to-in swing path, the ball will fly straight and to the left of your target. But it will not slice. So if you hear your problem is that you swing to the left, it isn't. The problem, if you are slicing, is that your clubface is open at impact.

That said, an out-to-in swing does certainly exaggerate your problem. For one thing it costs you time. When you swing to the left, the club is coming down on top of the ball and, if you are like most people, your hands aren't that fast, so you have less time to square the clubface. If, on the other hand, you make a bigger shoulder turn and get the club on a wider arc, you have much more time to square the clubface before it is too late.

The thing to remember is that the path of your swing does not cause your slice. If you feel as if you are cutting across the ball, it is only because the face of the club is open. And, as I've said, it becomes worse and worse the more you do it. The more the ball goes right, the more you swing left. The more you swing left, the less time you have to square the face and the steeper your swing becomes. Then your slice will be exaggerated.

The whole deal here is to get your clubface

Only one thing causes a slice—an open clubface at impact.

square at impact. Let's assume you have a neutral grip, your hands turned neither too far to the left or to the right. If this is the case you can assume that the back of your left hand is a mirror image of the clubface. So, if the back of your left hand is facing the target as the club strikes the ball, the clubface will be also. So you'll hit a straight shot.

Note, too, that if the back of your left hand isn't going to mirror your clubface—if you don't return your left hand to a square position at impact—the only way you can hit a straight shot is by adjusting your grip to compensate. This is the way everyone plays golf. Even the best swings have compensations built into them to make up for these mistakes. The key is to have an even number of compensations so that they cancel each other out. And, of course, the fewer compensations, the better hope you have to become a consistent golfer.

Okay, enough of the explanations. By now you should have a clear picture of just what kind of swing shape leads to you hitting a slice. There are seven main causes of a slice and each has a cure. Here are the cures:

1. Back of Left Hand

When you have a particular problem in your swing, you have to change your feel. Here, the feeling is that you are hitting the ball with the back of your left hand. If the back of your left hand faces the target at impact—or even a little before impact as a feeling—and your grip is fairly neutral, there is no way you can hit a slice. So if your clubface matches your grip and your left hand is facing the target at impact, the ball has to go straight.

To get the correct feeling in your left hand, pose at impact. Get the feel. Feel like you are rotating your left forearm as the club swings through impact. It is a combination of uncocking your wrists with the rotation of your arms. Ben Hogan called this move "supination," but think of it as moving the clubface from open to square to closed.

Focus on your left hand if that sounds a little confusing. The more you turn your left

hand on the downswing so that the palm is facing out away from you, the more you are squaring the clubface. The more you turn your left hand so that the palm is facing toward you, the more you will leave the clubface open. So you need to feel your hand turning square, almost to the point where the palm faces upward. That's a hook swing, but not a bad feel to have—at least in the short term—if you have been slicing the ball.

Here's another thought. If you slice the ball, either your hand is not turning to square the clubface or it is turning too late. So feel as if your hand has turned before you get to the ball. Rotate that left forearm counter clockwise—that is really what your release is. Practice at half speed to get the feel. Take it to the extreme so that you can, in time, hit only straight shots or hooks. Bye-bye slice.

The importance of this move in any good golf swing can be judged by the fact that this is one correction that you will use with every one of the following cures to ensure that your slice is gone forever.

2. Weak Grip

If you have a weak grip you can square the back of your left hand at impact and still hit a big slice. But the problem is easy to spot. If you are squaring your left hand at impact and you are still slicing, then your grip is too weak.

And, of course, the solution is simple. Turn both your hands to the right on the handle of the club, so that you can see at least

Posing impact helps you feel where your left hand should be as you hit the ball.

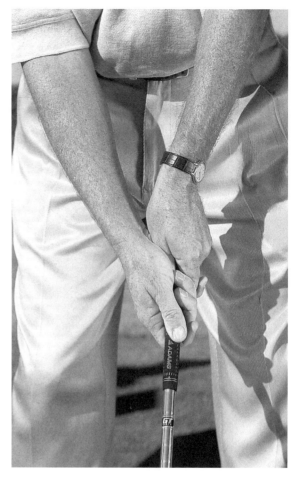

Strengthening your grip—turning both hands to the right—can help rid you of your slice.

three knuckles on the back of your left hand as you look down at address. The palm of your right hand should always face the palm of your left hand.

A stronger grip makes it easier for you to turn the back of your left hand over as the club moves through the impact area—all because your hands don't have so far to go to get the clubface square as it contacts the ball.

Be aware, too, that most people in need of

a stronger grip fail to strengthen it enough. So strengthen it more than you think you need to, at least initially.

Watch also for any tendency you may have to regrip the club just as you move it away from the ball on your backswing. I see so many people move their hands back to their original weak positions early on the backswing.

Again, at least in the short term, go for

exaggeration here. Turn your grip over more than you think you need to at address, then turn your hands as early as you can on the downswing in order to square the clubface. Turn them too much. Hit a few hooks. Then try to ease back to the middle ground.

3. Overly Upright Action

If you are trying to rotate and square your left hand as described above, but can't do it, the problem isn't likely in your grip. There is something wrong with your swing. In all likelihood, you are swinging the club on too upright a plane.

Upright swings tend to make your arms reverse rotate—clockwise—on the downswing. Here's what happens. When you swing the club straight up and down with your hands and arms, your arms will reverse rotate so that the left arm turns under on the backswing, then rotates the opposite way on the downswing. The end result is that the clubface is blocked open at impact.

The cure, yet again, is to move your problem to the other end of the scale. Fix your upright action by swinging the club more around your body on an arc. That's the feeling you want to foster, as if you are making more of a baseball swing.

Practice this with your club held at, say, hip level. Hold the club off the ground and make your swing. Feel how the club works its way around your body rather than up and down. It's more of a circular motion than a pendulum motion. Gradually lower the club

When the club is on too upright a plane, you are likely to hit a slice.

down to the ground while trying to maintain the feeling of the clubface closing at impact.

Practice, too, off a sidehill lie with the ball above your feet. This naturally flattens your swing plane without any effort from you. Try this with your eyes shut, focusing on the clubhead. Again, feel the more rounded, inside-to-inside swing you are making. Feel how your right hand works over your left, closing the clubface as it moves through impact and into the follow through. Do that consistently and the ball will soon be flying

Swinging with the club off the ground can help you feel the proper closing of the clubface through impact.

Teeing the ball higher than normal will help rid you of a tendency to hit down too much.

not from left-to-right but from right-to-left. This is a much more powerful shot.

On the course, you can practice this move by teeing your ball up extra high. This will force you to round off your swing if you want to make solid contact. It is unnatural to hit down on a ball that is teed-up high.

You can even—if you don't mind people staring at you on the range—try hitting a few balls while kneeling. I'm not sure I recommend this exercise too highly though! If you're like most people you don't want to look too goofy. Still, this exercise has the desired flattening effect on your swing. The more the golf club swings around your body on an arc, the more likely the clubface will square up at impact.

4. Rock and Block

Every good golf swing involves a turning of the shoulders and hips on the backswing and through swing. *And I mean turning.* Not tilting, which has the effect of steepening your swing.

Golfers who tilt rather than turn are also prone to have a disastrous reverse pivot— your weight moving to your left side on the backswing then to your right on the down-

A reverse pivot—your weight moving left on the backswing, then right on the downswing—is one of the worst moves in golf.

swing. If you rock and block, your left shoulder is going under too much on the backswing, with the right shoulder correspondingly going up too much. Then the opposite happens as the club swings down. The right shoulder goes under too much as the left shoulder moves too high. You need to turn your shoulders more level to the ground. If you are bent over too much at address, you will naturally tilt your shoulders more than you should. So stand a little taller to make your turn a little flatter. The feel you need to foster is one of your left shoulder staying up as it turns behind the ball on the backswing. As this happens your hips should turn very little, basically maintaining their original position. If your hips slide out over your right foot on the backswing, (and I'm assuming you are right-handed) your shoulders will tilt for sure.

When you get your body to turn more level instead of tilting it will be so much easier for you to get the feeling of your arms swinging the club around your body on an arc. Your shoulders just have to turn more level.

To get the right feel, practice this little exercise without a club. Stand as if at address. Then put your left hand on your right shoulder and your right hand on your left shoulder. Now try to turn your shoulders as close to level as possible, both back and through. Try to turn back so that your shoulders are all the way over a line that is opposite your right foot and perpendicular to your target line.

swing. Your weight should, of course, do just the opposite in a good swing; move to your right side on the backswing, then through onto your left side as the club swings through the ball.

So this time it isn't your hands and arms that cause the steepness in your swing. This time the problem starts with your body, which is *tilting* rather than *turning*. Ideally, your shoulders should turn on their axis. The bend from your hips you introduce at address should be the bend you keep throughout the

This exercise helps you turn your shoulders on a more level plane.

Turn until your shoulders are over your right foot.

"In, up, and over" is a common swing shape for a slicer.

5. In, Up, and Over

A swing path that is in, up, and over is another way you can get steep coming down. In fact, it usually stems from an overreaction to making an upright swing. In a misguided attempt to prevent that downswing steepness, it is easy to think that moving the club on a flatter plane to the inside on the backswing is the solution. It isn't. Such an inside move only forces you to lift the club to the top of the swing and become even more upright on the downswing. You will thus be forced to hit "over the top" of a backswing that was too flat and too much inside.

It goes like this. Your turn may be closer to level and your swing flatter due to the early inside move, but unfortunately you get too flat on the takeaway, lifting the club to the top and coming down "over the top" of your backswing on too steep a plane. So the end result is that you're in the same place on your downswing as you would have been if you simply took the club straight up on your backswing. You just got there in a different way.

The solution is to feel like you are reversing your loop. On the takeaway swing, move the club up and out, away from your body. From the top of the backswing, feel as if you are dropping the club to the inside. (That's the opposite swing shape to the one you had previously.) This will feel like you are swinging the club in a figure 8. If anything, you will soon be hooking the ball.

"Out, up, and in" is a good swing shape to practice when you are bothered by a slice.

6. Fanning the Face Open

Fanning the clubface open is a problem that has always perplexed me. You would think that if someone was fighting a slice, the last thing they would do early on the backswing is open the clubface. I don't know what people are thinking. But it happens. They just do it. So it needs to be fixed.

There is a giveaway with this fault. If I see a pupil set up closed—aligned to the right of the target—with his or her hands ahead or too high at address, it's a pretty good bet that the club will go inside and open up too quickly on the takeaway. Fanning the club open can, however, stem from all kinds of address positions, orthodox and otherwise.

If your swing shape is good and you still

Hands too far forward at address invariably lead to the club being "fanned open" on the takeaway.

hit too many slices, the problem could be that you are simply rotating the clubface too much away from the ball. In effect, you are opening the face too much and giving yourself that much further to go in order to square it again through impact. The clubface should gradually open on the backswing and gradually close on the downswing. In other words, the clubface should be square to the arc of the swing at all times, from start to finish.

Try to swing the club square to your arc on the way back, rather than rotating it open. "Eight o'clock" is a good check point. Move the club back so that it faces the ball longer. Make that your swing thought. Even if you initially overdo it, it is very much a step in the right direction.

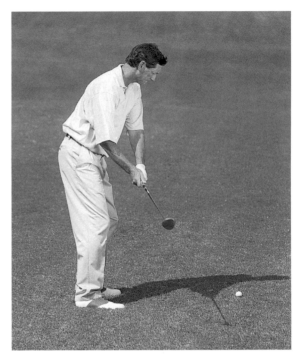

At "eight o'clock" the clubface should still be facing at the ball.

7. Cupping the Left Wrist

This mistake can stem from the "fanning" motion I described above. Or it can be caused by a sideways hinging, rather than an upward cocking, of the wrists as the club moves back. If the club starts back too flat on the backswing, it will usually be lifted to the top of the swing in such a way that the left wrist will be in a "cupped" position.

Whatever way this happens, the net result is that the face of the club becomes open at the top of the swing—the toe end hanging straight down. This is caused by the "cupping" of the left wrist. The way to fix is this is to get your left wrist flat at the top, which will help move the clubface into a much

squarer position. Ideally, your left arm, your left wrist, and the clubface should all be on the same plane at the top of the swing. This is easy to do if you swing the golf club up and around on plane on the backswing.

If you have a longer and looser than average swing—and you are slicing the ball—check your left wrist at the top. A cupped left wrist goes with a loose and long swing. (A bowed left wrist is generally a feature of a shorter, tighter swing.) Getting the clubface square at the top of the swing greatly increases your chances of squaring the clubface at impact.

Above: "Cupping" the left wrist puts the club in a toe down position.

Right: Your left wrist, left arm, and the clubface should be parallel at the top of the swing, as Mark O'Meara demonstrates here.

Hooking

There has always been an irony about hooking the ball in golf. Most golfers I know would love to be able to hook. That's because, generally speaking, a hook is a better player's fault. I just don't see many weaker golfers hitting too many hooks. Yet, on the other hand, I can't think of too many top players who have not fought a hook during some time in their careers. Ben Hogan was plagued by a hook for years. Lee Trevino developed his own unique swing method as an anti-hook

device. And Jack Nicklaus played nearly all of his best golf with a fade, as he tried to eliminate the left side of every hole he played. The common factor with these golfers, of course, is that they all were extremely talented players. The pattern that leads to great ball-striking is first to learn how to draw the ball in order to fix your slice, then learn how to make sure your draw doesn't become a hook.

A hook, for all that it is rarely desirable, at least has a strength about it. A slice, in contrast, is relatively weak. If you don't believe me, watch how each ball reacts when struck into a headwind. A hooked ball tends to have a lower, more boring flight. A sliced ball is nearly always higher and less penetrating.

Just exactly what a hook? For one thing, there is a difference between a hook and a pulled shot. Most of the time, a hook starts to the right of your target, curves in the air from right-to-left, and sends the ball left of where you want it to finish. A pull is often confused with a hook because it also finishes left of your target. Don't be confused. A pull is generally a straight shot that starts left and stays there.

There are four primary causes of hooking:

1. A swing that is too flat or rounded—the opposite of a slice swing.

2. A club that drops to the inside on the downswing, thus creating too flat a swing coming into the ball.

3. A loss of synchronization between your body, hands, and arms, with your hands and arms moving too fast in relation to your body.

4. Too strong a grip.

Let's look at each cause in turn.

Too Flat

Where a slicer swings the club on too much of a straight line, a hooker moves the club around his or her body on too much of an arc. In other words, the swing is too round or flat.

This tends to happen because of two rea-

Hookers tend to swing the club on too flat a plane.

sons. Either the flatness is introduced very early in the swing; or later from the top. If your swing is flat early the problem is in your arm swing or shoulder turn. Either or both will cause the flatness.

To combat a flat swing that is caused by a shoulder turn problem, make sure that at address you are bent over the correct amount from your waist. Concentrate on maintaining that posture as you turn, your left shoulder working under more on the backswing.

If your club swings on too flat a plane because of your arm and hand action at the top, make sure that your wrists hinge the golf club up on the backswing. And keep your hands and arms in front of your body as you swing the club up to the top of the swing.

Left: Keep your hands and arms in front of your body.

Above: Dropping the club from the top can cause it to get "stuck" behind you.

It is also important to get the correct rotation of your left forearm on the backswing, so as to get the club on plane as it moves up and back. This rotation allows you to make the same move in reverse as the club moves down.

Drop from the Top

If you get to the top in good shape—on plane—but then drop the club to the inside it will get "stuck" behind you. This tends to a better player's mistake. Even Tiger Woods has to watch out for it on occasion.

When this happens you are forced to flip your hands over the ball through impact, with the club swinging on too much of an arc and the face closing too rapidly.

Instead of dropping the club from the top, focus on the re-rotation of your left forearm—down and into your side. That will get the clubhead more out in front of you and shift the clubshaft onto the correct downswing plane.

That's not all. From the top feel as if your hips are moving more laterally than they have been. Get your weight shifting from

Rotating your left arm down and into your side from the top of the swing will get the club down in front of your body, like Jesper Parnevik is doing here.

Turning your hips on the downswing keeps your swing in sync, as Sergio Garcia shows here.

your right heel to your left big toe as you start the club back down to the ball.

All of the above encourages you to hit the inside part of the ball so that your draw starts to the right of the target and not to the left.

Poor Timing

Poor timing happens when your hands and arms move too fast in relation to your body.

At impact your hips are square to the target, rather than open as they should be. So you need to focus on speeding up the rotation of your lower body as the club swings through.

Focus on your hips. Their turning is what keeps your timing correct on the downswing. Correct timing is essential to squaring the clubface at impact. Your hips must turn through. If you hang back and your hands and arms keep going, the clubface will close too much and you will hit that hook.

Strong Grip

A strong grip is easy to fix, although, like all grip changes, it can take some time to get used to.

You know your grip is too strong when your swing plane is good, your body is rotating properly with your hands and arms, yet

If your hips don't turn, your hands will close the clubface and cause a hook.

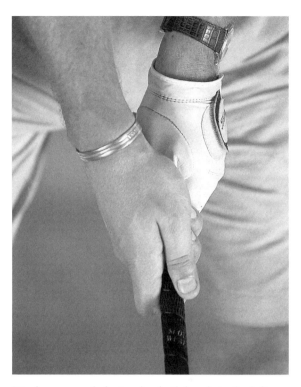

Weaken your grip by turning both hands to the left.

you still hook the ball. The problem must be your grip.

Weaken your hold on the club by turning your hands—both of them—to the left on the club. You should be able to see one or perhaps two knuckles on the back of your left hand; your thumb just to the right of center on the grip. Your right hand should be placed more on top of the club than before. Your right arm will also feel higher.

Quick checkpoint: the "Vs" formed by your thumbs and forefingers should point up toward your right cheekbone.

One last thing. Don't neglect your grip pressure. If you are hooking the ball, it may

The "V" formed by your thumbs and forefingers should point at your right cheek.

be because your hands are simply too active through impact, thus closing the clubface down too quickly. Active hands are often the product of a loose grip. So hold on tighter. This will restrict your hand motion.

Pushing and Pulling

A push is a shot that starts right and goes straight right. A pull starts left and goes straight left. A lot of people think a slice is a push and a hook is a pull. Not so. The difference is that pushes and pulls have no curve to them.

Indeed, pushes and pulls are probably the most misanalyzed shots in golf. When a ball flies to the left of where you want it to go, it is easy to think you came "over the top" of the shot. Coming over the top means that your swing path is out-to-in, with the face square to that path. So the ball starts left and stays there.

And those factors—your swing path and the angle of the clubface—lead to your pushes and pulls.

When you hit a push or a pull, there are four possible causes:

1. Swing path,

2. Aim,

3. Ball position, or

4. Club fitting

Usually either the path of your swing or the clubface has caused the ball to start to the right for a push, or to the left for a pulled shot.

Studies have shown that 75 percent of the time, the reason why a shot starts in a particular direction is the point of contact on the clubface. The rest has to do with swing path.

It's so important to determine what causes the push or the pull. Is it the path? Or is it the clubface? Or is it a combination of both?

Usually it's the clubface. If your pushes or pulls have any curve to them they become, in effect, push-slices and pull-hooks. Either way, this is a definite indication that your clubface has caused the push or the pull. If your ball starts to the right or to the left and your divot is pointed in the direction in which the ball started, then that is an indication that the path of your swing has had at least some impact on making the ball push or pull.

The reason you swing in the wrong direction is because you curve the ball in the opposite direction. In other words, you swing to the left because you tend to slice to the right. You want to get the ball in the fairway.

You'll swing to the right for the same sort of reason. If you tend to hook, you aren't going to swing to the left. No one ever swings towards his problem. In theory, you could have a swing path out to the right—ordinarily a push swing—but if the clubface is closed enough to contact the outside half of the ball, you can still hit a pull. This happens quite frequently, so pay attention.

Don't fall into the trap of thinking a push or a pull stems from a swing path problem. To be sure, however, check your divot holes. If your problem is your swing path, the direc-

The direction of your divot hole shows you where your shot started.

tion in which your divot hole is pointed will be the direction in which the ball started.

Swing Path

If your aim is good and the ball is positioned correctly within your stance, yet you are still pushing and/or pulling, and your divots point to the right or left of your target, then your swing path must be off. Either you are swinging too much out-to-in or in-to-out.

You see it all the time on the television. When a pro pushes or pulls a shot, the first thing they check for is the direction of the divot they just took. You need to do the same.

Again, look at your divot holes for information. An in-to-out swing is going to hit behind the ball. An out-to-in swing will hit in front of the ball. An in-to-out swing will

cause the divot to point to the right. An out-to-in swing's divot will point to the left.

If you are swinging too much from in-to-out, you need to feel like your backswing is a little straighter away from the ball. To get the path going through straighter, put more emphasis on turning your body through the shot. You may even have to feel like you are swinging the golf club more to the left in the through swing.

If you are swinging too much from out-to-in, you need to swing a little more out to right field. In order to do that, it is very important that you make a good turn behind the golf ball on the backswing. This will give you the opportunity to swing the club more to the right on the downswing. There are no guarantees, however. A good backswing turn alone isn't enough to guarantee you a good shot or that you will swing to the right on the downswing. You need to also feel like your back is facing the target at the start of the downswing, and that your hips are moving a little more laterally before they start to turn through. This will get you swinging from the inside. One symptom of a pulled shot is a "backing up" of the hips as you swing through impact and into the follow through.

If your clubface is creating the pulled shot—straight divot, ball starts way left—then a closed clubface is causing the pull, which is usually accompanied by a little bit of a hook. In that case, the problem could be your grip, your closed face at the top, or any other number of causes. But primarily, if the clubface is closed and thus causing a pull, you have the same characteristics as someone who hooks the ball. So you need to work on the same corrections for hooking the ball.

The opposite is true of the push-slice. You need to refer to the corrections for a slice.

When your hips don't move laterally enough you will tend to hit the outside of the ball and hit a pull.

Aim

All that said, the first thing to check if you are pushing or pulling is your aim. You could be aiming where the ball is going. Right-handed players especially have a tendency to aim to the right. Watch for this.

And don't just check your feet. Maybe your clubface is aimed to the right or to the left. Maybe your shoulders are opened or closed. You have to make sure *your whole body is aligned.* Whether you are pushing or pulling, your feet, your knees, your hips, your shoulders, your arms, your eyes, and the clubface all need to be properly aligned.

Ball Position

Ball position is a much underrated aspect of your golf swing—if one can call the position of the ball relative to your feet part of the swing. But think about it. Because you swing the club on an arc, the ball needs to be precisely placed within your stance. The golf club swings on an arc around your body from inside to square and back to the inside. The clubface is square for only a brief moment and hopefully that's where you've placed the ball.

Check that the lie of your clubs is right for you. If the lie is too upright, the heel will be off the ground; too flat, the toe will be off the ground.

If you are pushing or pulling, the first thing to check is your aim, as Mark Brooks does here.

If the ball is too far back in your stance, impact will occur too early in the swing and you will push the shot to the right. If the ball is too far forward, impact will occur too late and you'll pull the shot to the left. Ball position is very important when correcting a push or a pull.

Club Fitting

A pull or a push can also be caused by the lie of your golf club. If the club is too upright, the toe will stick up too much in the air at address and you will tend to pull. If the club is too flat, the heel will lift up off the ground at address and you will tend to push.

Again, take a look at your divot holes for clues, specifically their depth from toe to heel. If your divots are toe-deep, then your club is too flat for your swing and you will tend to push to the right. If they are heel-deep, then your club is too upright for you and you'll likely hit pulls. This comes down to the fact that the club just doesn't fit you properly. Or, at least, doesn't fit your swing.

Let's take a closer look at each.

Pushing

Like the slice, a push is a ball-flight error. The two are closely related in as much as the ball finishes to the right of the target for both, but a push differs in that it is a straight shot compared with the curve of a slice.

You can be laid off at address . . .　　on the takeaway . . .　　halfway back . . .

A push shot, then, starts to the right and flies straight. This can stem from something as simple as a faulty ball position—too far back in your stance—but the most common cause is the club is "laid off" at some point in your swing.

You may have heard this term before. And if you're like most golfers you probably think it refers to the top of the backswing; the club pointing to the left of where you want the ball to go.

If you think that, you'd be right. But only partly. That's the trouble with so many golfing clichés or terminologies. Like political rhetoric they don't always give you all the facts.

The truth is the club can be laid off at any point in your swing. Even, as we'll see, your setup isn't immune. What remains constant

is where the ball tends to finish. No matter where you get the club in a laid-off position, you will tend to block your shots to the right of where you want them to go.

There is one difference, however. Poorer players tend to lay the club off on the backswing. The better players invariably wait until the downswing.

That said, laying the club off has nothing to do with your body. Or your feet. Or your knees. Or your shoulders. The problem is caused by your hands and arms. Which helps us. If we know what the problem is, we know where to look to fix it.

When you get the club laid off, it is lagging behind your hands at any point in the swing. The result is that the club comes into the ball late with the clubface open to where

at the top . . .   halfway down . . .   and approaching impact.

you want the ball to go. Unless you "save" the shot by flipping your hands over the ball through impact, you will hit the shot straight right.

That, of course, is no way to be consistent. If you don't use your hands enough the ball will still finish to the right. If you use them too much you run the risk of smothering the ball to the left, or, even worse, hitting a quick duck-hook. Neither, as I'm sure you can imagine, is particularly desirable.

There are six places to check if you have the club laid off: at address, on the takeaway, halfway back, at the top, halfway down, and approaching impact. As you can see from the pictures on pages 84-85, the common factor with these check points is that the hands out-run the club. Let's look at each in turn.

At Address

Because there is little or no movement involved in your address position, this is the easiest laid-off mistake to spot . . . and to fix.

The problem is that your hands are too far forward in relation to the clubhead. If your hands are as little as an inch too far ahead, you are already an inch laid off. The key here is to get "centered."

Move your hands back until they are directly in front of the zipper on your pants. If we assume that you are hitting an iron shot, your hands should still be ahead of the ball. But only just.

In effect, your arms and shoulders should form a close to perfect isosceles triangle in front of your body.

At address, your hands should be in front of the zipper on your pants.

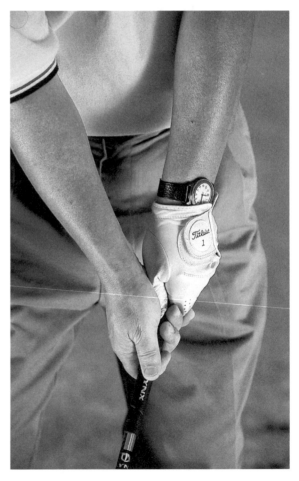

If your hands are too far forward, you are laid off.

| From address . . . | cock your wrists up. | Then turn and rotate your left arm. |

On the Takeaway

The problem with the takeaway is, invariably, one of confusion or, at the very least, a misconception.

The key, as I've said, is in your hands and arms. If you are laid off on the takeaway you have almost certainly turned your hands in a clockwise direction rather than cocking your wrists up. That's how your wrists should work in the swing. They cock up as your body turns into the backswing. Think of it as the same movement you employ when casting a fishing line or hammering a nail into a piece of wood.

To encourage that feel in your wrists, try this simple exercise. From address, cock your wrists up so that the club is in front of your chest. The relationship between your hands,

arms, and club is now essentially what it should be at the top of your backswing.

And that is all your hands and arms have to do. If you turn your body from there and start to rotate your left forearm, you'll be in a perfect position in the takeaway.

Halfway Back

When the club is laid off halfway back on the backswing, the problem can usually be traced to the left wrist. If it bows back the club will be too far behind you and the shaft too horizontal. If the club feels heavy to you halfway back, then you can be pretty sure you are laid off.

Your aim is to make the club feel lighter. As the club moves back, move your left arm a little closer to your body. Feel as if your hands

Above: Halfway back, your arms should be about in the middle of your body, like Vijay Singh.

Right: As you near the top of the swing, your hands and arms should be out and away from your body, as Paul Runyan shows here.

are more underneath the shaft and the club-head. At this point the club shaft should be above but parallel to its original angle at address. If you achieve this, your backswing is off to a great start . . . but you're not done yet. Keep reading.

At the Top

If you are laid off at the top of your swing, the evidence is clear to the naked eye. The golf club will be pointed left at the top of the swing. This also is often a point of confusion.

Of the students who have come to me with this problem, most think it is caused by not turning enough on their backswing. They make their normal backswing and find that the club is pointing way off to the left—laid off. So, understandably, they try to turn their shoulders more to get the club "on line" at the top.

But wait. Remember I said that getting the club laid off is a hands and arms mistake? Turning your shoulders more isn't going to help.

Think about it. Assuming you are set up

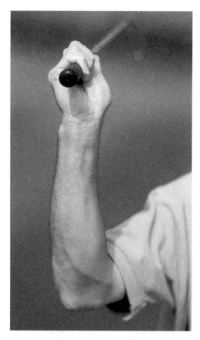

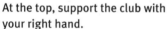
At the top, support the club with your right hand.

Yes, like Stuart Appleby.

No.

squarely to your target and you then have turned your shoulders 90 degrees on the backswing, then the club should be parallel to your ball-target line at the top.

If that isn't the case, you are laid off. And turning your shoulders to, say, 120 degrees isn't going to alter that fact. You're still 30 degrees laid off, and you'll still hit the same block shots to the right if your shoulders lead the club through. All you've done is conceal your original fault.

The key, as I've said, is in your hands and arms. Focus on the relationship between your left arm and the club. Ideally, you want your left arm, your left wrist, the club shaft and the clubface to be right in line with one another, no matter how much or how little you turn your shoulders.

You can achieve this by feeling as if your right hand is "tweaking" the club to the right at the top of your swing. When you do this feel some firmness in your position; your hands underneath the club. You will feel as if the club is lighter when you are supporting it properly at the top of the swing and heavier when it is laid off to the left.

Focus also on your right palm and the clubface. One should mirror the other. If your palm and the clubface are parallel, you can support the club easily in your hand. If your hand is bent back, your wrist breaking down, the shaft and clubhead will sag off to the left. Laid off.

Halfway Down

If you are laid off at the halfway down point, the problem—and the solution—is simple. All you have to do is focus on lowering *the handle* of your club (not the clubhead) from the top of your swing.

As your hips make a slight lateral motion to initiate the downswing, make a conscious attempt to lower *the handle* of your club while you rotate your left forearm into your body. Think of nothing but that, at least initially. Don't pull the handle down; let it fall. Gravity will help you with this once you get started. The clubhead will follow the lead of the handle, keeping you on plane. If the head starts down first, the handle and your hands won't necessarily follow and you'll be laid off.

Into Impact

Even at the point of impact, it is still possible to get the club laid off. Test yourself. If you tend to hit the ground behind the ball or your divots are non-existent or thin at best, it is certain that you are laying the club off late in the swing.

The byproduct of this move is an alteration in your posture. It won't take long for you to get tired of hitting the ball fat, so you will instinctively pull up so as to give the club and yourself more room in which to hit the ball. That's the easiest way to rise up as the club swings through.

Those are the symptoms. Here is the cure. Feel as if the bend in your hips at address stays constant throughout the swing. The

Lower the handle of the club as you start the downswing.

feeling may even be that you are increasing your bend as you start the club down from the top of the swing. Yet again, as you do this the key is to keep the club out in front of you by re-rotating your left forearm in tune with your body.

Focus on rotating your body and left forearm as the club swings into impact and, as it does so, square the back of your left hand. When you do this the back of your left hand and the clubface will square up as you hit the ball.

Of course, doing this is a lot easier if you

Maintain your posture, as Chip Beck does here.

Then rotate your lower body. Tiger Woods does this better than anyone ever has before.

maintain your posture throughout the swing.

Your hands will to some extent follow the lead of your body. But if you are used to blocking the clubface open at impact, you must think of squaring the back of your left hand at impact, just as if you were fixing a slice. If you continue to get the golf club into a good position coming down, that squaring motion will start to become second nature, thereby eliminating at least one thought. Less thought; better shots. Sounds like a good combination to me.

Pulling

Like a hook, a pull is a shot that ends up to the left of the target. The difference between the two is that a pull, unlike a hook, has no curve to it. The ball flies straight. Which

sounds good. But the problem is that the ball flies straight to the left of where you want it to go.

If your ball starts out left of your aim and you know that the path of your swing is not the problem because your divot is pointing straight to your target, then a closed clubface that hits the outside of the ball is the cause of the pull.

When this is the case, there is usually a little bit of hook-spin in your swing, too. Look first at your grip. The problem could simply be that your hold on the club is too strong (your hands turned too far to the right). Then again, the clubface could be closed at, say, the top of your swing because the club has turned in your hands on the backswing. Or it could be any number of factors that have caused the clubface to close.

If the clubface is closed and causing your ball to pull, then your mistake is similar to that of someone who hooks the ball. No surprise there.

The various hook corrections we have already covered may be all you need. One thing to look out for, however, is that many golfers who fight a pull misanalyze their shots and think that they are "coming over the top" every time they hit a pull. That isn't even close to the truth.

In fact, better golfers whose bad shot is a pull have the golf club coming into the ball too much from the inside and not too much from the outside.

That may seem illogical but is easily explained. The most common mistake—which in turn leads to the club coming down into the ball too much from the inside and behind you—is to have the club "across the line" at the top of the swing.

When the club is across the line at the top, it is technically on an upright plane. But not for long. When the golf club starts down from the top of the swing, it flattens and gets stuck behind you. Next thing you know, you instinctively stay "behind" the ball, your hands flip over, and the clubface hits the outside part of the ball, sending the shot pulling to the left.

Most people think that the golf club should be pointing right down the target line at the top of the golf swing. If you swing the club all the way back into a parallel position, that is indeed correct. But, anytime the club is short of parallel it should actually point off

to the left if it is to be on the correct swing plane.

As I said, having the club across the target line means that it is on too upright a plane—and this can happen at anytime in the swing, just the same as laying the club off. Many golfers are aware that they can get the club across the line at the top. But the real questions are: what caused the steepness and when did the swing first get off plane?

Just as you can be laid off anywhere in the swing, you can also be across the line anywhere from address to the finish. This typically leads to confusion in those golfers who are across the line at the top. In an effort to "fix" the problem, they shorten their backswings. But that never works. Getting across the line is not a body turn mistake.

No, just like laid off, across the line is a hands and arms problem. So any corrections you make to fix it have to relate to your hands or your arms or both.

There are a few check points you can use to gauge whether or not you are on plane during your swing—across the line, remember, means you are too steep. Which, in turn, leads to you flattening the club too much on the downswing. Which, in turn, leads to the club getting stuck behind you. Which, in turn, leads to your hands flipping the club over through impact.

Note that this "stuck" position is the same one a better player gets into when he or she blocks the ball far to the right. The difference is that when the club is stuck behind you and your upper body stays back, your hands flip

At address, the triangle formed by your hands, arms, and shoulders should sit right in front of your body.

At address, your arms should be hanging directly down from your shoulders.

over and you hit the outside of the ball. Result? A pull to the left.

That same club position with the upper body leading through will cause the opposite shot—a block to the right. In any case, this isn't where you want to be. You have two options, neither of them attractive: You can stay back and hook the shot, or you can move forward and block it straight to the right.

Let's take a look at the places in the swing where you can be across the line. It starts at address and works its way to impact.

At Address

If you want to hit a straight, or close to straight, shot, it is critical that your address position be neutral. If your hands are too low, or too far back, at address, the club is already in a sense across the line. If your hands are too far forward, or too high, at address the golf club will move back too much to the inside at the start of the swing. Then it has to go up at some point. And when it does you will be across the line at the top.

To avoid all of the above, make sure that

Too flat a takeaway can lead to you being across the line at the top.

Your wrists must hinge up on the backswing. Here the hands are turning instead of the wrists cocking up.

your hands are sitting right in front of your body at address, with your arms hanging directly down from your shoulders. The triangle formed by your hands, arms, and shoulders should be right in front of your body.

On the Takeaway

If your clubshaft is off the correct swing plane—either too upright or too flat—then it is a battle (usually a losing one) to get it back on plane. If the club starts back too flat and underneath the plane, chances are it will

over-correct and be too upright and across the line at the top.

Equally, if the club is too upright on the takeaway, the club is already across the line and quite possibly will continue to be as you complete your backswing.

A proper takeaway is one that combines the upward cocking of your wrists and the rotation of your left forearm, with your shoulder turn. Either too much or not enough wrist cock or rotation of your forearm will get the club off plane.

Most commonly, I see players get across

In a correct takeaway the clubhead is coming up and in at the same time.

If the clubshaft is too upright at this stage, you are already across the line.

the line at the top as a result of an inside take-away where the right wrist bends back and takes the club to the inside too quickly. So make sure that your wrists hinge up at the start of your swing.

Halfway Back

If the clubshaft is too upright in the middle of your swing, you haven't rotated your left forearm enough and the club will already be across the line. If the shaft is too flat at this same point, you have rotated your hands and/or arms too much and the club will likely start to get more upright at the top of the swing. And upright equals across the line.

In general, the more the golf club is out in front of your body and not swung too much across your chest and behind you, the better your chances are of getting the club to the top on the proper plane.

To achieve this, your left arm needs to start rotating at this point on the backswing. And, just as important, that rotation needs to continue all the way to the top of the swing.

The left forearm rotates to get the club on plane on the   backswing,

downswing,   and through swing.

At the Top

If you are across the line at the top of your swing, you will probably see the clubhead out of the corner of your left eye as the shaft points too much to the right.

And, once again, this is a simple point of misunderstanding for many golfers. They mistakenly assume that across the line is the same as "too long." In reality, swinging the club across the line at the top of your swing—or, for that matter, anywhere else in the swing—has nothing to do with making too long of a backswing.

Being across the line, just like being laid off, stems from a problem with your hands and arms. When the club swings back to the top, it should be parallel to the target line at the same point that the club is parallel to the ground.

If the club swings past parallel, the club should then point across the line. If your clubshaft is across the line at this point, your left arm is likely too low and too much across your chest, with your right hand too much on top of your left hand.

Ideally, your left arm, wrist, the clubshaft, and the clubface need to be in line with one another, no matter how much or how little you turn your shoulders.

Take practice swings in front of a mirror. Feel the correct position at the top of your swing. Concentrate on how the weight of the club feels. If it seems very light, you are probably across the line. If the club is heavy it is probably laid off. Somewhere in between those two extremes is where you want to be.

If you are across the line at the top, you may be able to see the clubhead out of the corner of your left eye.

Halfway Down

If you are across the line at the top of the swing, then it is almost inevitable that the problem will persist into the downswing. The reverse problem that is.

Assuming you are across the line at the top, the club will begin to flatten on the downswing. Halfway down you should be close to being on plane. Unfortunately, the flattening process continues on and, by the time you hit the ball, the club is too flat and stuck behind you.

This position is similar for someone who

Your hips should move a
little laterally on the
downswing.

If your hips are "backing up" through impact, you are almost sure to pull the shot.

pushes shots to the right. In fact, those players tend to move in front of the ball with their right shoulders before hitting the ball to the right. Those who pull stay back, flip their hands over, and catch the outside of the ball.

The cure for both is similar. Both the pusher and the puller need to get the club down in front of their body on the downswing. To do this rotate your left arm down and into your body from the top of the swing. With the club out in front of you, it will come into the ball on the correct arc and your hips can rotate through the shot, preventing the clubface from closing too much on impact. Having the club out in front of you

as it approaches the ball is still no guarantee that you will not pull the shot to the left. But it's a great start.

Into Impact

Focus on these thoughts. Make sure that your hips move a little laterally on the downswing. This will help you hit the inside of the ball. Keep those hips rotating through impact, too. This will delay the closing of the clubface enough to ensure that your hands don't flip over and hit the outside of the ball. One symptom of the chronic puller is a "backing up" of the hips through impact and beyond.

On the downswing the hips move laterally and turn through the shot, as seen here with Steve Elkington *(left),* and Tiger Woods *(right).*

Thus, the correction for the clubface pull or pull hook is similar to that for the clubface push or push-slice. The only thing that is different is that to eliminate the pull you need to turn your body through a little more and a little faster. In both cases, you need to get the golf club coming down in front of you.

Even in his forties, Seve Ballesteros has one of the best short games in golf.

4

Short Shots—A Test of Nerves

hile it is true that most people would rather spend the vast majority of their time hitting full shots—whether on the course or on the range—a good case can be made that the short game is the most important aspect of golf.

It depends, though, on your priorities. If your aim on the golf course is to shoot the lowest score you can, then you better find a way to get the ball into the hole in less than three shots from, say, 80 yards. A huge percentage of the shots you hit in a typical round of golf are struck from inside this range. So the better you are with your short shots, the lower you will score.

Of course, it's not that easy. For even the best players, any deterioration in nerve or skill or technique tends to show up first in the short game. The great Spaniard Seve Ballesteros is the only obvious exception. In his early forties he still has the great touch and skill around the greens that made him a great champion.

For the rest of us, however, advancing

years usually mean more missed putts and fewer up and downs. Which is another good reason why a good short game is worth working on—it can improve your golfing longevity far past your longer-hitting but clumsy peers.

The reason for this is simple. While a good short game technique is no less important than in any other part of the game, it is also true that, generally speaking, a short pitch over a bunker tends to induce more nervousness in a player than, say, a full-blooded drive to even the narrowest of fairways.

Why is that? Because short shots *are short*. They don't require full swings at full speed. You can't simply go ahead and swing, allowing your—hopefully!—hours of practice to take over. No, short shots ask different questions of your golfing ability.

To play a short shot well, you need more than good technique. You need nerve. And you need that indefinable quality—*feel*. How hard should you hit a 60-yard pitch? How big a backswing should you make? I can't tell

The high pitch is one of the most useful shots in the game, and Tiger Woods is great at this shot.

you for sure, but I can make an educated guess. Only you, after practice and experimentation, will know with absolute certainty to these questions.

Pitching—So Important

I have always been a fan of the pitch shot. It has a lot going for it in so many ways. For one, it is such an important shot to be able to play.

Think about it. In every round of golf even the best players miss, oh, at least three or four greens. On maybe two of those misses they will be able to chip onto the green; the ball flying low and running up to the flag. On the others they must pitch the ball into the air.

If you can't pitch the ball into the air you are stuck. You can't give yourself a chance to get up and down in two shots. You probably won't get down in three some of the time. So one bad shot can lead to you wasting two, three, or four shots. All because you couldn't loft the ball in the air and onto the green.

Being able to play a pitch from anywhere will also give you confidence. Golfers miss greens for a number of reasons. Poor technique. Hitting the wrong club. Misjudgment. And, here's the most important: because of a fear of missing.

Why are they afraid? Because they know that, should they miss the putting surface, they are going to be faced with pitching the next shot onto the green. And that is a shot they just don't have.

For all those reasons, I recommend you work on your pitching game. It doesn't take much. You're not going to use up a lot of energy hitting fifty pitch shots. And sound pitching technique is the first step towards

Missing a green in the "right" place gives you the best chance of saving par. Even Tiger has his hands full here.

building a better full swing. The pitching swing is simply a shorter and slower version of the full swing.

Saving Shots

Here's another reason why pitching and a good all-around short game is so important. This is the area of the game where it is easy to waste or save shots. It's hit or miss, whether you are pitching, chipping, or exploding from a bunker. There is no in-between. Having said that, I prefer to look positively on golf's short shots. Think of them as opportunities for you to make up for a bad shot or to bail yourself out of a tough situation.

Short shots are your scoring shots. They dictate the range of your scores, much more than your long game. Like I said, even the best players in the world don't hit all the greens. On average they hit maybe thirteen, so face the fact that in every round of golf you will miss greens. The key is missing in the right place so that you have a reasonable chance to get the ball up and in. Where you miss is a big part of having a good short game. You need to be in a position where you have a decent shot.

Of the three short shots, pitching is the most important. You can't play proper golf without being able to pitch the ball in the air. Bunker play is simply a variation of pitching. And chipping is really an extension of putting.

That said, though, make pitching your last resort when you miss a green. From just off a green you want to putt whenever you can. Your worst putt is almost always better than your worst chip. When you can't putt, chip—putting the ball in the air for only a short time. And when you can't chip, pitch—the ball flying higher so it spends more time in the air. Note, too, that "higher" doesn't necessarily mean "high." Pitch the ball high in the air only when you absolutely have to—from the rough, over a high bank, or to very fast greens.

Pitching—What Goes Wrong

The most common bad shot in pitching is the complete duff. Whether through bad technique, nerves, or poor execution, golfers tend to hit pitch shots fat. We've all done it . . . I know I have.

Just as in your long game, a fat shot is caused by a swing that is too steep, or the bottom of the swing occurring too far behind the ball. You can also hit fat shots because your clubface is closed, the leading edge digging too much into the ground.

Thin shots are a reaction to fat shots. You swing the club into the ball and your instincts tell you that you are going to hit the ball fat. So you pick up either with your body, arms, legs, or hands. Whichever, the end result is that you hit the ball around its equator and send it scurrying across the green. A "sickening knee-high fizzer" was how the late golf writer Peter Dobereiner used to describe such a shot.

Thin pitches set off a chain reaction. Maintaining your height in an attempt to eliminate the "pull-up" isn't enough.

Here's why. If you don't get the club com-

Putt from off the green whenever you can. Here I am putting with a 3-wood to get the ball rolling.

ing down and hitting the ball where the bottom of the swing is, you'll hit a shot fat. As soon as you've done that a few times, you will find it impossible to maintain your height, and you don't want to in this instance. If you are going to hit behind the ball you are better off lifting up. Just hope you lift up the right amount.

Basic Technique

A good pitch shot should feel like the club-face is open enough so that you are sliding it under the ball. It should also feel like a level swing. You don't have to hit down a lot on a pitch shot. All this does is make it harder for you to be precise at the bottom of your swing. If you are even a little off you'll hit a shot fat. So you want to sweep the shot off the ground, and slide the club under the ball with the face open.

Stand *slightly* open.

You only need to make a small swing, so your lower body should be out of the way. To do this you want your feet aligned a little left of the target. But *not* your shoulders. If you play a really high cut-pitch, you might have to open up everything, but in general only your feet should be open just enough to get your hips out of the way.

Address the ball with the face of the club slightly open. You should also take a slightly wider than normal stance, and stand a little farther away from the ball. This will lower your hands and your center of gravity, which is good because it gives you more loft.

As for ball position, you want your hands no farther forward than level with the ball. In fact, a little behind is fine to add loft to the shot. Over time, as your pitching improves, you will find that a lot of this stuff becomes instinctive.

But I do have one hard and fast rule: Do not—ever—grip down on the club. Hold the grip where you would for a full shot. The more you choke down on the club, the closer

Above: Stand slightly open—your feet aligned to the left—for a pitch shot. For a very high pitch, stand farther away with your hands lower.

Below: Lowering your body and your hands will add loft to the club for a higher pitch shot.

Your hands should be no farther forward than level with the ball. Tiger Woods shows a correct address for a high pitch.

Hold the club as you would for a full shot, just as Tiger does here.

you will stand to the ball, and the more you hold the shaft of the club upright. An upright club will cause you to hit the ball low. Which isn't what you want to do.

Once you are set over the ball, make sure you maintain the openness in the clubface as it moves away from the ball. At the end of your backswing the toe of the club should be pointing up to the sky, as opposed to the face turned down to the ground. A shut face stems from not rotating your hands or your arms. Or too strong a grip. Rotate that face open so that you have loft on the club. If you do this, sliding the club under the ball will become a lot easier.

At this point you're probably wondering how much of a backswing to make. That is a question I am always being asked by my students. The answer is, "I don't know." Not for sure anyway. While there isn't much of a range in a swing this short, just how much of a swing you need to make in order to hit the ball, say, 50 yards is something *you* have to find out for yourself. It's something *you* need to practice.

Imagine you are swinging on the face of a clock. Swing the club back to nine o'clock then through to three o'clock (whatever length shot you have, make your back and through swings the same). Measure how far the ball flies.

The toe of the club must point upward on the takeaway, as mine does here *(above left),* and downward at the end of your backswing, as Tiger's does here *(above right).*

Now make longer and shorter swings, measuring how far each allows you to hit the ball through the air.

At the end of only a few minutes you will have a reference point for every length of shot. You'll have a 30-yard swing, a 50-yard swing, and a 70-yard swing. Not only will that help you with the execution of any pitch shot, any doubt about how much of a back-swing to make will be eliminated from your mind. That's important. Poor pitching results from doubts in the mind, just as much as poor technique does.

One symptom of indecision is a deceleration of the clubhead through impact. But, to me,

If the clubface isn't open enough the club will be de-lofted and the ball will come out low.

that is an overrated problem. Deceleration doesn't cause poor pitches. Granted, if you accelerate through, you have less chance of hitting behind the ball. Or it may make up for the fact that the bottom of your swing is behind the ball. But deceleration in itself doesn't make you hit the ball fat. In fact, for some shots it actually looks like the player is decelerating the club.

So don't worry about deceleration through impact. Focus instead on creating the correct angles in your swing. As long as you don't stop completely at the ball, the angle should be your only concern.

Bad Shot: The Fat Pitch

Those who have trouble with pitching are typically those who don't take advantage of the loft on the club. Pitching is simple in that—because the wedge has loft inbuilt—all you have to do is swing your arms back and forth and the ball will fly high.

If you can't do that, you are delofting the club somewhere either at address or during the swing. When this happens the sharp end of the club tends to dig into the ground and cause a fat shot. You want the club to glide; not dig.

To encourage that gliding motion, you need to add loft to the club as you swing. An easy way to do this, of course, is to simply open the clubface at address. Then, if you make your regular swing, the ball will fly higher. You can also add that loft during the swing. The key is the point in your back-

A de-lofted clubface will also have a tendency to dig into the ground too deep and cause a fat shot.

swing where the shaft is close to horizontal. When you've reached this point, the toe end of the club should be pointing to the sky. That's an open position, from which you can happily slide the clubhead under the ball to produce the high shot you want. This shot should feel as if you are brushing the top of the grass with the back of your wedge.

Bad Shot: The Bladed Pitch

The bladed pitch is really a reaction to hitting too many fat pitches. Just as in your full swing, if you do it too often you eventually

If you open the clubface properly the club will glide easier under the ball.

Your posture must remain constant throughout the swing, as Tiger's does.

get tired of it. And that is the point where you are going to lift up and catch the ball halfway up. Never good.

The cure for the bladed pitch, of course, is the same as the cure for your full swing. Focus on your posture. Try to maintain the same body angles from your setup at address all the way through your swing. Do that and you will start making consistent contact with the ball.

There is another possible problem. You could be using too much wrist action and not enough arm motion in your swing. Which means not enough arm swing. That combina-

tion leads to you "scooping" the shot at impact; the clubhead rising and catching the middle of the ball.

Fix this by going back to your basic chipping motion, especially with reference to your wrists. Swing your arms back and through, trying to keep your wrists firm. Once you have that feel—and are hitting short shots solidly—introduce a little opening of your wrist on the backswing. This will allow you to hit the ball a little farther and a little higher.

A word of warning: if you are like most students I see, you are already using too

Too much wrist action can cause you to "scoop" the shot.

To counteract "scooping," swing with firm wrists, as Tiger does here.

much wrist action in your swing, whether you are hitting a pitch shot or a full shot. So try to use as little wrist action as possible. All you need is a little opening of the right wrist on the backswing. Anything else is surplus to requirements. *Less movement is better.*

Chipping

I see a lot of pupils get confused when they move from pitching to chipping. It's easy to mix up the two. For example, I see people pitching and choking way down on the club. That's no good for a pitch shot, but perfect for a chip.

When you chip you want to choke down on the club. You want to stand closer to the ball. You want your feet close together. All of those moves shift your center of gravity up and forward. A chip shot requires more of a descending blow. All you need to do is make solid contact. You also need to take loft off the club. You don't want to add it. So move most of your weight—around 75 percent—forward onto your front foot.

The most common mistake in chipping is "scooping"—trying to lift the ball up in the air with your hands instead of allowing the loft on the club to do its job.

Forget the scoop. You don't want the ball

to fly very high anyway, so why use your hands to lift it up more than necessary? In chipping you want a little bit of a descending blow. That's why your hands need to be ahead of the ball at address and at impact. You want to contact the ball, then the ground. You're not trying to hit a high shot.

Many times, in fact, even if you hit a chip lower than you meant to, it'll turn out pretty good. Generally, you can't hit a chip shot too low. Only when the ball doesn't carry to the point where you want it to land is the shot too low. Equally, you can't hit a chip shot too high. But if you are hitting too high, take a less lofted club that'll hit the ball lower with no effort from you.

As for the stroke itself, you need to make only a very short swing. Short back; short through. Create momentum in the club

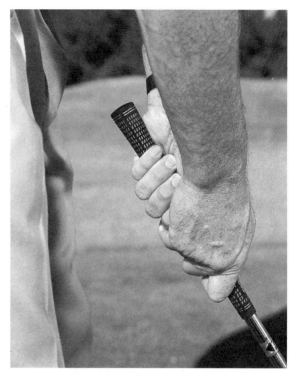

For a chip shot, grip down on the club.

Never try to "lift" the ball with your hands. Too much hand action is never good when chipping.

When chipping, set the club upright, the heel a little raised.

with your arms, not with your wrists. A little wrist action won't hurt; a lot of wrist action will.

Bad Shot: Fat Chip

Almost every poor chipper uses too much wrist and hand action. Do that and you are condemned to scooping the shot. You'll lose the correct angle at the back of your left wrist, hit up on the shot, and hang back on your right side a little. All of these actions move the bottom of your swing back, away from the hole.

When that happens, you are condemned to hitting the ground behind the ball. That's no way to be consistent, or hit the shot solidly.

Focus on your angles at address. Every aspect of your setup should help you hit down on the ball a little.

Place the ball back of center in your stance, your hands ahead of the ball. Your stance should be a little open and your weight forward. Stand close to the ball and, this time, choke down on the club a little. Set the club upright, the toe on the ground, the heel a little raised.

All of the above, combined with a stiff-wristed stroke, will make this the simple shot it should be. It is, after all, nothing more than an extended putting stroke.

Bad Shot: Thin Chip

Which brings me to thin chips. This should be a hard shot to hit, but yet I see it all the time. People scoop the shot with their hands, miss the ground and catch the ball on the upswing.

Such a shot is, in fact, a close relative of the fat chip. When you hit fat, you are scooping

A thinned chip should be difficult to achieve if you hit down and through.

and hitting behind the ball. Or you have a good angle of approach, but not a good setup. In other words, your ball is not far enough back, or your hands are not far enough forward, or your right shoulder and your center line are not far enough forward to let you hit the ball first.

One last point. Don't become too involved with club selection when chipping. Choose a landing area, then select a club with enough loft to land the ball on that spot without any manipulation from you. In other words, *keep things simple.*

Always have a target area where you want your chip shots to land. Bruce Lietzke is chipping here with a fairway wood.

Too short a follow through is a common fault in bunkers.

Bunkers

Fact one: Many golfers are scared when they see their balls go into bunkers.

Why are they scared?

Fact two: Because they don't think they can get the ball out in less than two strokes.

Why are they so lacking in confidence?

Fact three: Because they don't commit to making a big enough swing and don't use their sand wedges properly.

The biggest mistake I see in this last fact is that people don't have the clubface open enough, or the ball forward enough in relation to their feet. Then, just to compound this, they don't follow through. They hit the sand and stop the clubhead at the ball or just beyond.

Those are the facts. Here's the story.

Take a look at your sand wedge. It is designed in a very specific way. The bottom of the club (the flange) acts like a rudder as it moves through the hitting area, which should, in theory, prevent you from digging too deep into the sand.

The idea is that the ball flies out of the bunker on a cushion of sand. It's that easy. If you can get just one little patch of sand out of the bunker, the ball will come out too. Let's face it, you don't even have to hit the ball!

But, all too often, that end result isn't so

Try to hit the sand behind the ball, just at the point where the club hovered at address.

straightforward. All too often, things go wrong.

Here's what happens. When a ball doesn't come out of a bunker either you have not made enough of a swing, or you made a big swing but have not used the club in your hands to your best advantage.

In the first case, it comes down to physics. When you hit down into sand, the clubhead slows down. It just must. There's nothing you can do about that. So, because the sand resists, you need plenty of speed in the clubhead to get the ball and the sand out of the bunker and onto the green. If you don't have that speed, the ball won't come out. Nor will the sand, although that is less important!

Then there's the other scenario. As I said earlier, bunker play is a variation of pitching. So you need to hit every shot with the face of your sand wedge open. That's the way to take best advantage of the club's flange.

If the clubface is square or shut as it hits the sand, the leading edge is going to dig too much into the bunker and the ball won't fly far enough, if at all.

But that's getting ahead of ourselves. Excessive digging happens later, after the initial mistakes have been made.

I see this in new students all the time. They come to every greenside bunker shot with a basic lack of understanding of what it is they are trying to do. If that sounds like you, follow these simple instructions. They are your first steps toward improving your bunker play.

First, open the face of the club. Then take your grip. Do it in that order. Don't take your grip and then turn the clubface to the right. If you do that, the clubface will return to square during your swing. So it's open face, then take grip.

Second, play the ball forward in your stance, opposite your big toe. Put it there because you want to hit *behind the ball.* The ball is in a sense too far forward for a normal shot, but you don't want to hit the ball. You want to hit the sand behind the ball.

Third, wiggle your feet into the sand a little and open your stance to the target. You want a firm base for this shot, but know, too, that as your feet get lower you must make other adjustments to compensate. Choke up on the club a little to allow for the fact that you are closer to the ball.

Fourth, know in your mind that you are going to have to make a positive swing. Your feet are dug in, so that will inhibit any pivot in your legs. The face of your club is open, as is your stance. And you are hitting into sand. So you better hit hard.

Fifth, aim to hit the sand behind the ball. Don't get too specific. Two, three inches, or whatever. But know that the more sand you take the more you will have to accelerate that clubhead through impact.

Sixth, make a full swing along the line of your toes. And follow through. That's key. You should make equal back and through swings, just as if you are hitting a pitch shot. At least three-quarters back and through.

Do all of the above and the ball will come out. Every time. Believe me.

Varying Your Distance

Okay, you are getting the ball out of the sand every time. That in itself is a huge improvement, but now you want to get a little more sophisticated; you want to hit the ball close

Make a full follow through on your bunker shots, as Mark O'Meara shows us here.

to the hole. Which means you have to learn how to vary the distance of your shots.

Short shots are the toughest shots for most people. The tendency is to revert to a short swing—make that too short—or take too much sand and not enough follow through.

Forget all that. When you play a high, short shot, make a little slower swing. Hit the sand at the same place behind the ball, but lower yourself at address. Take a wider stance. Toe both feet out a bit. Both knees, too. Lower your hands. You want to lower your center of gravity and put more loft on the club.

The lower you are, the softer the shot will be. The taller you stand at address and during the swing, the longer the shot.

Bad Shot: Buried Lie and Can't Get Out

Your ball is half-buried in the sand, so you can't play your regular splash shot. This happens occasionally, so you better be ready to cope with it. What to do?

Realize first that in order to dig the ball out you have to use the digging part of the club. What you need here is a steeper angle of attack into the shot. You need more wrist action in your back and through swings. You need more of an up and down movement in your arms. That will help you make the vertical swing you need in order to make the club dig into the sand.

If the ball is badly buried, square your clubface up a bit to help it dig into the sand. If it's really bad, you can even shut the face and, in effect, stick the club in the sand behind the ball. Really. Just stick it into the sand and leave it there. You can't really hit hard enough either. If you give it everything you have, at least you know the ball is coming out. Yes, you won't have much control. But that isn't your priority here anyway. Just be sure to allow for the fact that the ball will run a long way on landing.

Soft Sand

Soft sand can be intimidating because it looks and feels like it is easy to hit too much sand and leave the ball in the trap.

Don't worry. Your plan is to hit half an inch beneath the ball. No more. Dig your feet into the sand—let's say down two inches. Choke up on the club by the same amount. If you don't you'll tend to hit too much beneath the ball, take too much sand, and not be able to get the ball out.

Soft sand also offers more resistance so swing through with more commitment and make a bigger follow through.

Hard Sand

With hard sand you need to hit down more. Use most or all of the club; don't choke down. Lift your arms more and cock your wrists more. Keep the clubface closer to square to minimize the chance of it bouncing on the hard sand and into the middle of the ball.

That's your swing. No go ahead and hit it!

Downhill Lie

Make most of your adjustments at address. You need to get your body parallel with the slope. So lean into your left side.

Because the lie is going to make the ball fly lower than you would like, you need to swing more across the shot. So that you can get a sharper angle of approach, you need more of an out-to-in swing path from a downhill lie.

Open the clubface as much as you comfortably can and swing harder, too. All to make up for the down slope.

Uphill Lie

Depending on the length of shot you want,

From a buried lie, make an upright swing, then stick the club in the sand.

Make sure you take enough club to clear the lip as Ben Crenshaw has done here.

Turn your body through as Mark Brooks does here to make sure you catch the ball before you hit the sand.

there are a couple of ways to play uphill lies.

If the shot is a short one, tilt your body with the slope. Then swing down the slope and up it again. The combination of slope and the open clubface will prevent you from hitting the ball very far.

If, however, you need a bit of distance from an uphill lie, set up with your body tilted into the slope. This time you want the club to hit into the slope, so as to take loft off.

Fairway Bunkers

Fairway bunker shots are difficult shots for the simple reason that they do not give you any margin for error. You have to hit precisely at the ball. So the only adjustment you need to make is to move the ball back in your stance.

Hang on though. If you do this the ball will fly lower than normal. To compensate for any loss of height, choose a club with more loft. Assuming, of course, you have a lip in front of you to clear. Hit the ball and the sand at the same time, while looking at the top of the ball or the front of the ball. Put your emphasis on turning through; not back. When you turn through, that moves the bottom of your swing forward. Which is good. You definitely don't want to hit behind the ball.

As you walk toward a green, take note of the contours on the putting surface.
Here Tiger Woods and John Cook have a look at what lies ahead.

5

Putting

One of the curiosities of golf is that everyone who plays the game likes to hole putts, yet few are prepared to work hard at what is, statistically at least, the most important aspect of the game.

If you don't believe me; consider this. On a 72-par golf course you are, according to old man par, supposed to use your putter thirty-six times on the 18 holes. Half your even-par score! If that isn't enough to get you to at least consider taking a little more time on the practice green, I don't know what is.

But there is, of course, a lot more to putting than mere technique. Nowhere else in the game does the mental side of golf play such an important role. Witness the number of players out there who suffer from the yips—which is provoked largely by a fear of missing—if you doubt that fact.

Confidence is a good putter's greatest ally. But putting with confidence is easier said than done. You can't assume a truly confident attitude just by saying to yourself that you are confident. There's more to it than that.

On a day-to-day basis, confidence on the greens is usually the result of holing a couple of useful putts early in the round. Most great putting rounds start out that way. Not many are the result of three-putts on each of the first three greens!

Visualization can be a big part of every golf shot, but it is particularly useful on the greens. Start thinking about your next putt as soon as your ball lands on the green.

As you walk towards the putting surface, take note of its contours. This can help you judge the general direction and amount of break you will have to play on the upcoming putt, especially for long putts. Perhaps just as important, this mental focus gets you thinking in a positive manner about just what you have to do to get the ball into the hole or at least very close. Negative thoughts are something you want to avoid at all costs.

For example, it is better to think how and where you are going to hit the putt rather than to think what you must not do. In other words, say to yourself that you should be up to the hole rather than you must not be short.

That said, the best way I know of building both confidence and a positive attitude on the greens is through sound technique. If you have belief in your method, that sureness will transfer itself to your mind and body.

Technique — Distance Control

It was Ben Hogan who said that golf is two different games—hitting the ball and putting. And he was right; those two aspects of the game are wine and cheese. In putting there is far more room for individuality than there is in the full swing. You can break all kinds of rules and still be a great putter. As long as the ball goes into the hole, it doesn't really matter how you do it. Look at Isao Aoki. This Japanese star won tournaments all over the world with a kind of toe-in-the-air stroke that was definitely all his own.

But here's my point. While there are many different putting styles, there are common factors in all the great putters, no matter how they choose to get the job done.

Here's two: Great putters all have good distance control, and they all hit the ball solidly on a regular basis. Those two factors go together. There may be two parts to every putt—distance and direction—but distance is the most important.

Think about it. How many times have you left, say, a 40-foot putt six feet short? Or knocked it eight feet past the hole? Quite a few times, right? Now consider how often you have hit the same length putt six feet left

Distance control is one of the most important aspects of putting.

or eight feet right of the hole. I'll wager not too often. Distance control is a lot harder than working out the line, especially on longer putts.

Take care though. Studies have shown that around 85 percent of putts are missed on the low side—and 100 percent of the people who hit those putts thought they had allowed enough break. So, most of the time, allow more break than you first think. On second thought, make that a lot more break than you first think.

Most putts are missed on the low side—so allow for more break than your first think, especially if you use the long putter like Bruce Lietzke.

That said, I tell my students to work hard to roll the ball the same distance time after time. Once you can do that, you can putt. Distance is that important.

Think about it. Almost every putt has some sort of break in it. Being able to read the break will help you make the putt. And good green reading can only be done successfully if you have at least a pretty good idea of how hard you have to hit the ball. If you can't hit the ball the right speed, it is difficult to figure out how much break you need to play. So distance is also important in that.

Then there is the fact that almost every first putt is followed by another putt. So, if you hit the ball the right distance your next putt will be shorter.

What is the optimum speed for a putt? I like to see every putt roll at a pace that carries the ball to about 12 to 18 inches past the cup—if it should miss, that is. This pace keeps the ball on line and, again, makes the amount of break easier to gauge.

Of course, distance control is less important on short putts because they tend to have less break in them. But distance has a role to play there, too. While you won't be off as much in your distance control on a short putt as you would be on a long putt, you still have to choose your line. You're still asking yourself two questions: What's the line? And how hard should I hit the ball? Read on.

Different Strokes

There may be many different ways to putt, but there are really only two shapes of strokes employed by the world's best putters. You can swing straight back to straight through, with the clubface square. Or you can open the clubface on the backswing, then close it again on the through swing. The best thing about these two methods is that each keeps the compensations down to a minimum. But, if you are willing to practice enough to groove the stroke, there are other ways to get the job done.

You could aim to the left with the clubface open. You could aim to the right with the clubface closed. Any combination of face alignment and swing path is fine—as long as it starts the ball on line. Great putters have used all of these techniques.

The late great South African Bobby Locke was one of the greatest putters ever and he hooked all his putts. PGA Tour player Billy Mayfair cuts every putt and makes more than his fair share. Just about the only thing you don't see is someone putting with the heel of the club off the ground.

There are other "no-nos" in putting. You don't see any player putt with their head forward—nearer to the hole—of the ball. The head is either over the ball or behind it. Like Jack Nicklaus. He keeps his eyes right over the line and turned his head to the left to look directly at the hole.

Which brings me to the eyes. Everyone has their eyes either over the ball or inside that line; never outside. Most people stand square or open, rarely closed; although Gary Player was one player who stood square—very successfully, too—for a long time.

Then there are wrist putters and arm putters. Nowadays most players on tour putt with their arms and shoulders. That's because the greens are so fast. But not so long ago, when the pace of the putting surfaces wasn't what it is today, men like Billy Casper did well with wristy strokes. Players needed this wrist action to get the ball to roll better on top of the grass.

The bottom line? Putting is a very personal thing.

Bad Putt—Too Much Movement

Like good putters, bad putters have a lot in common. They all move their heads a lot. They don't stay steady. They move their bodies rather than letting their hands, arms, and shoulders swing the putter. They have too much lateral body movement during the stroke.

Good putters keep their heads still, almost to the point of listening for the ball to drop on short putts. Bad putters don't do that. They peep to see where the ball goes even before it rolls. Some almost have leg action, which make their strokes inconsistent. Such a little swing doesn't need body motion.

Good putters have a smooth tempo. Poor putters tend to rush the transition from back to through stroke. Which is true in the full swing, too, of course. That's why, while I am always prepared to allow any of my pupils some leeway when it comes to their putting, there are limits. I am not, for example, going to let someone move his or her upper body excessively during the stroke.

I see this all the time. An incredible number of people use an excess of upper body movement in their strokes. Typically, the right shoulder comes around to face the hole. Even if you want to see where the ball goes

Too much body movement in your putting stoke can only lead to inconsistency.

before you hit it, fight the impulse to look.

Instead, focus on maintaining the triangle formed by your shoulders and arms at address. Keep this position firm all the way to the end of your follow through. Ben Crenshaw, who has long been one of the finest putters of the game, does just that. I'm hard pressed to come up with a better role model for you on the greens.

Excessive upper body movement shows up most in short putts. Any breakdown in your upper body sends the ball—mostly—to the left of where you want it to go. If you miss a lot of short ones on the left side, focus on following through to the hole. Let your putter head follow the ball square as much as it can. On really short ones, you can even let the putter head cover the hole.

Ben Crenshaw maintains his triangle from start to finish, and he is one of the all-time best putters.

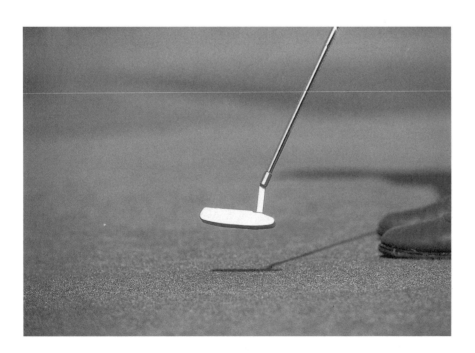

On all putts, make sure your putter head faces at the hole after you hit the ball.

On short putts, feel like
you stroke through right
to the back of the cup.

Grips

You really have three choices with putter grips. You can hold the club as you would any other. You can use the reverse overlap grip where the first finger of your left hand overlaps the little finger of your right. Or you can putt cross-handed, left hand below right hand. I call this "upside down," and some people call it "left hand low."

Whichever you choose, make sure both your thumbs are straight down the shaft. Your palms should face each other with your right palm facing straight at the target. Or you may have both hands turned out equal amounts.

The Left Wrist

The left wrist receives a lot of attention in putting. I hear a lot of commentators say how putts are missed because, "He broke down in his left wrist."

Maybe.

I think this left wrist stuff is way overblown. I've seen too many great putters whose left wrists break down as they strike the ball believe this is a problem. It is far more important that you strike every putt with the proper amount of loft on the putter. If you do this, it really doesn't matter what your left wrist is up to. Besides, if your left wrist does break down before impact it may affect the putt; but after? No way.

Reading Greens

When you read a green you are looking for slope. Every green has some slope, so that the water can drain off it. When a green is built, there is typically at least a half inch to an inch of slope for every ten feet. So there is always some fall one way or another.

Most greens drain four ways. Look for the way water would drain off. That's the way your ball is going to break. Imagine you are

Don't worry about your left wrist breaking down a little after impact. Mark O'Meara made one on 18 to win the Masters with this stroke.

And cross grain putts will break more or less than usual.

Putters

With all the different designs you see in your local pro shops and golf stores, there are really just two basic putters: center-shafted and heel-shafted. A heel-shafted putter is better for those who prefer the Crenshaw-like open-to-closed stroke, where the toe of the putter opens and closes back and through.

A center-shaft putter is better if you like to move the putter head straight back and through.

If you like to forward press with your hands just before starting the putter back from the ball, you don't want a lot of off-set on your putter. Your press is going to de-loft the club so you need a bit of loft there to compensate.

Every putter has loft. Three or four degrees loft is about right for optimum roll. If you have too much loft the ball will bounce too much, flying off the putter. Not enough loft has the same effect but in a different way. The ball bounces too much because you are driving it into the ground. In general, a putter with less loft is best suited for faster greens. On slower greens, you'd be best served by a putter with more loft.

Where your hands are in relation to the clubface at impact determines how much loft you need to have on your putter. If you are comfortable with your hands way forward, you need more loft on your putter. If your

dumping a big bottle of water on the green. Where would all the water go? That's the way the putt will go, too.

Grain is different, depending on where you are. Bermuda grass greens have a lot of grain. Bent grass grows straight up. Bermuda grows toward the setting sun, or toward water, or away from mountains. But always at an angle.

Pay attention to the grain. It affects the break and speed of a putt. Down grain putts are faster. Into the grain putts are slower.

If you have trouble reading a putt, try to imagine where water on the green would run off. The ball will go the same way.

hands are back—relatively speaking—you need less loft.

As for the length of your stroke: Just as in pitching and chipping, try to make the swing the same length on both sides of the ball. Make it a pendulum motion. That's the best way I know to have consistent contact between club and ball.

Be Realistic

If you're like most people, you are too hard on yourself when it comes to putting. Your goals are simply unrealistic. Take it from me, a machine can't make too many putts from ten feet.

I try to define great putting by putts per round. But your ball striking and chipping are part of this equation, too. To be a good putter you need to be a good chipper and a good course manager. If you miss greens in bad spots, you won't be able to get your chips that close to the hole, and then you will not be able to make that many putts. One bad shot leads to another.

So set yourself some reasonable goals. Begin with trying to two-putt every hole. As you get better, try to lower that number. If you want to be a top amateur player you have to average less than thirty putts per round.

The Yips

Yips is a terrible affliction that starts with poor technique. Because you miss so much, doubt enters your mind, overriding anything sensible in your thought pattern.

To rid yourself of the yips, keep things as simple as possible. Take your hands out of your stroke. Move only your arms and shoulders. It should almost feel as if you are in a plaster cast.

Work on moving the handle back on a straight line, then let the clubhead release from the start of the downswing.

That's your starting point. Better technique leads to better club-ball contact, which builds confidence. The trick is letting that progression take place.

Playing the game well requires you to recover from a bad shot, as Arnold Palmer demonstrates here.

6

Playing the Game

If you are like most amateur golfers I have met, the following should sound familiar.

Ask yourself this question. How often do you walk off the 18th green feeling happy that you haven't wasted any shots during the round?

That's right, *never*.

Now, while the perfect round has yet to be played—and probably never will be—we'd all like to get closer to that ideal. And the best thing is you can do just that without hitting thousands of balls.

I'm talking here about playing golf, not swinging the golf club. The two are closely related, of course, but distinctly different.

A good swing is part of playing golf well—that's obvious—but it is only a piece of the whole equation. There is so much more to getting your ball around the course in the fewest number of strokes. If you get too wrapped up with your golf swing, it is difficult to play golf as well as you can.

Which is why I bring you a guarantee. If I were to caddie for you and give you advice on

every shot, your score would fall by, on average, five or six shots.

Don't get me wrong. I'm not talking about giving you a swing tip on every shot. That would only lead to confusion. No, all I'd do is give you strategic advice on things like aim, playing the percentages, laying up . . . that sort of stuff.

Think about your last round. How many times did you make a mental error? How many times did you choose the wrong club? Or hit the wrong shot?

Exactly. You probably made at least a few mental or strategic mistakes.

Without touching your swing, a good coach or caddie can knock those six shots off your score on an average day.

Perhaps most important, he or she will know the shots you can't hit. Those tend to vary, of course. For you it might be a bunker shot. For someone else it could be a half wedge from around 70 yards out. Whatever the case, if you keep away from the shots you feel least comfortable playing, your score will fall dramatically.

You'll enjoy your game more, too. All too often I see players put too much pressure on themselves to hit a great or at least really good shot. That's almost always a mistake.

Here is how I look at it. For every golf shot, there are, let's say, three possible results: good, not bad, and bad.

All you have to do is eliminate the "bad" possibility. "Good" is hitting the green. "Not bad" is missing the green in a place where you have a better than decent chance to get up and down. And "bad" is missing in exactly the wrong place, on the right of the green with the hole cut on that side, for example.

So, assuming you fail to hit your target, all you have to do is make sure you miss in the right place. Or, in other words, not in the wrong place.

That's really what playing the game is all about. Picking out the right club. Playing the right strategy. Teeing up on the proper side of tee. Knowing how to play uneven lies and bad lies. Knowing how to set up and knowing what your ball will tend to do.

You also have to be ready to deal with wind. Strong winds affect scores more than any other factor in the game. More than extremes in temperature. More than the speed of the greens. More than the height of the rough.

Another part of playing golf well is learning how to practice. Not just your technique, but also what you should do in certain situations. If you're like most players, you have a problem setting up a good plan and sticking to it no matter what happens on the course.

Strategy

Strategy is one word that covers a big area in golf, so I'm going to focus on a few of the basics. Here is what I call my Ten-Point Strategic Plan for Success:

1. Teeing Up

This is an easy one. Teeing up on the correct side of the tee can make even the most daunting drive seem a little bit more friendly to your eyes.

It's a simple principle. If the fairway is, say, 40 yards wide and you tee up in the middle of the tee, you only have 20 yards on either side into which to hit. If, on the other hand, you tee up on the far right or left of the tee you now have the whole 40 yards of fairway to play with.

Which side you use depends on where the trouble is. Let's say there are a lot of bunkers up the right side of the hole. Tee up on the right side of the tee so that you are, in effect, aiming "away" from the sand, thereby taking the trouble out of play.

Don't underestimate the importance of this simple move. Moving your ball as little as two yards on the tee can make a huge difference 250 yards down the fairway. So think about where you tee up, it can turn a difficult hole into an easy one.

You can also extend this plan into par-3s. If the pin is located, say, on the far right side of the green, tee up on the left side of the tee. This will "open up" the shot for you.

A word of caution at this point. Teeing up

If the pin is located on the right side of the green, tee up on the left to give yourself a better angle in to the flag.

missing on the left side will leave you with an easier chip. You'll have more room on the green to work with, which will make your chip shot or pitch shot that much easier.

Is this too negative an attitude? No. Most golf tournaments are lost, not won. Remember that fact. You don't often see someone romping home by making birdies on the last three holes. So play the percentages. In the long run that will be more productive for you.

It's common sense really. Play to your ability level. Don't attack unnecessarily. Play to your strengths. If you have a good short game, miss where you have a chance to get up and in.

2. When To Attack, When Not To?

The easy answer here is "pick your spots." The best do. Even Tiger Woods doesn't go for every pin.

But let's take my buddy Mark O'Meara as an example. Mark's staple shot is a slight draw, the ball moving from right-to-left in the air. That fact makes pins on the right side of the green less accessible to Mark than those in the center or left side.

On the other hand, someone like Colin Montgomerie, who hits a left-to-right fade most of the time, will have an advantage shooting to a pin on the right side, but feel less comfortable going at a hole cut on the left of the putting surface.

That doesn't mean Mark and Colin aren't trying to get the ball close to holes that are

on the left may give you a better chance to get the ball close to the hole, but recognize it as an aggressive play. When the hole is cut near the edge of a green, it may be more sensible to play for the center of the putting surface, especially if there is trouble on the short side.

So also pay attention to where you want to miss. In the situation I have just described,

Mark O'Meara is more comfortable drawing the ball.

less accessible for their ball-flights. They are. But if the penalty for missing is severe, they'll play for the middle of the green, two-putt, and move on. That's sensible. They will wait for a hole where they can be more aggressive.

So should you.

The only players who can attack every pin are those who can move the ball either way at will, or those who hit the ball so far off the tee they always hit a short iron to the green. I don't know many of those guys and, chances are, you aren't one of them. *Remember, play the smart shot.*

3. Under-clubbing

Most people overestimate their ability to hit the golf ball. They think they can hit it longer than they actually do. Those are facts.

A fade is Colin Montgomerie's staple shot.

According to the pros I teach, this is the number one mistake they see in pro-ams.

Take a look at any green on your home course if you don't believe me. Where are most of the pitch marks? That's right; at the front of the putting surface. If you stood all day betting that each player will come up short with his approach, you'd make a lot of money.

Part of the problem is that few amateur golfers actually know how far they hit the ball with each club. And if they do, they take the wrong measurement. A pro measures the carry he will get with a particular club. An amateur measures everything!

That can have a huge effect on where your shots finish up. If the green has a hazard or trouble in front of it, the pro knows what club he needs to carry his ball onto the putting surface. The amateur is less sure. You might, for example, be able to hit a 5-iron, 180 yards total, but that might be 155 yards carry and 25 yards roll. So, to get your ball on the green, you may need to hit as much as a 3-iron. That's *need to*. Trouble is, you'll probably go with your 5-iron, come up short and be left with a tough chip. It's an ego thing.

The solution is simple. Find out how far you hit the ball with each club, both through the air and on the ground. If you don't know, you are guessing all the time.

In fact, you don't even need to measure your distances with *every* club. Two is enough. Let's say you typically hit your 8-iron about 150 to 155 yards and your 3-iron

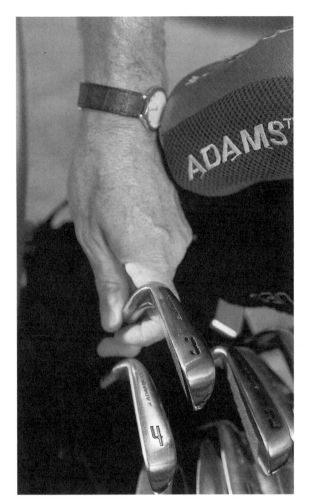

If in doubt over what club to hit, most of the time you would be better off with the longer one.

about 190 to 195. You can work every shot off those yardages. Use them as starting points.

For example, let's say you have 160 yards to the flag. In calm conditions that would be, for you, a 7-iron. But the shot is into the wind. So it's a 6-iron. But you start your calculations from your 8-iron.

4. Too Many Drivers?

You're on the tee at a long par-4 or a par-5. So it must be a driver, right? Not necessarily. Watch the pros on television. They don't hit that many drivers in a normal round of golf.

In fact, on a tight course they may hit only three or four. I've never seen a pro hit more than ten shots with a driver in a round of golf on the PGA Tour. There are almost always at least half a dozen holes where they hit a fairway wood or an iron instead. Those clubs have more loft, which gives more backspin and counteracts sidespin on the ball.

That's why you will tend to hit straighter shots with your more lofted clubs. Certainly they will have less curve to them. All of which makes a fairway wood or long iron from the tee a smart play nine times out of ten. A ball in play—albeit farther from the green—gives you more chance to make par than does one in knee-high rough.

Base your decision on whether or not to use a driver on the distance you can drive the ball in normal conditions. Also consider the shape and layout of the hole you are playing.

If we assume that you want to land your ball in the widest part of the fairway, let that fact determine what club you hit. If typically drive the ball 275 yards but the landing area is at 250, you have to adjust.

5. Pre-shot Routine

Under pressure, people get out of their rhythm. You see it in all sports. Anything that breaks your routine is a tell-tale sign

Hitting a lofted wood or a long iron as Fred Couples did here will give you a better chance to put the ball in the fairway.

that you are nervous or are having trouble with the situation. Usually this stems from your thinking of all the possible consequences rather than just playing the shot. If you're thinking about where you don't want the ball to go rather than the process that will send it where you do want it to go, you're headed for trouble. Most psychologists recommend that you stick with your routine.

Get yourself a pre-shot routine and stick to it every time.

Every time. Of course, it helps to have a routine in the first place.

Work on doing the same thing or things before every shot. Don't get carried away—you don't want to make it too complicated and end up playing too slowly—but a couple of practice swings, a look at the hole, and then proceeding is fine.

And work on your speed. Not just in your swing, but before each shot. We all have a routine or natural speed. Nick Price is a naturally quick person. He walks quickly and he waggles the club in a brisk fashion. So he swings quickly, too. On the other hand, Ernie Els is a lot less frenetic than Nick. He does everything a bit slower and his swing reflects that. So know yourself. You'll play better if you recognize your routine and stick to it no matter what.

6. Practice

It's a fact of golfing life that all of us are better either with the woods or the irons. It's hard—if not impossible—to be completely confident with both. The key is your swing plane. If you are an upright swinger you'll be better with your short irons. If you are a flat swinger you'll be better with your woods or with the ball teed up.

Former Masters champion Jose Maria Olazabal is a perfect example. His upright action makes him a supreme iron player and probably one of the poorer drivers of a ball among the world's best golfers.

That said, it has always seemed a little odd to me that most golfers spend most of their practice time working away on their favorite clubs. That makes no sense.

In your practice, work toward the opposite of your current tendency. If, for example, you like the ball teed up, practice with the ball on the ground. That will help you develop a steeper angle of approach. If you like the ball down because your swing is steep, practice with the ball teed up.

Teeing the ball up will help most people. Specifically, slicers. If that sounds like you, practice with the ball teed up. That will help you round off and level off your swing, making it more shallow.

Since most ranges don't have much grass on them it is better to tee up. Give yourself a decent lie to make it more like it will be on the course. Not only does it help your swing, it makes it closer to what you will get on the course.

If you are more concerned with your inability to score well rather than to swing well, focus on your short game. Most people would benefit from work on their short games. About 80 percent of your shots are hit from within 100 yards of the hole and that's where most amateurs could really use improvement.

7. Crosswinds

Golf is an outdoor sport, so there is no escaping wind. The eternal question is: do you fight the wind or use the wind?

The answer is obvious. On every shot you

must try to let the wind help your ball towards the hole rather than blowing your shots off-line.

To that end, think of your shots as breaking putts. The old theory on the greens is that every putt is straight as far as you are concerned. You simply aim for a point and let the slope and/or grain take the ball to the hole.

Sounds simple . . . and it is. Or can be. Think of your full-shots into a crosswind as long putts. Pick out a target at the point where you think the ball will be blown back to the green or fairway.

Sometimes, of course, that is easier said than done. If the wind is pushing at your back—the hardest wind for any golfer—your tendency will be to adjust your swing to accommodate the wind, rather than simply aiming left or right to allow for the breeze.

Aim is most important. And again, teeing up on one side of the tee can help neutralize the wind. You want to hit into the wind as much as you can. If it is blowing left-to-right, tee up on right and hit to the left.

That's true most of the time anyway. But there is an exception to the rule. If the wind is blowing left-to-right but there is little or no trouble on the right side, tee up on the left and blast away.

In other words, let circumstances dictate your tactics.

8. Into the Wind

Most golfers underestimate the effect of a headwind and come up short of their target.

This is an extension of the under-clubbing problem I see in too many pupils.

Then there is the mental side of playing into the wind. If you're like most people you've been over a shot, doubted your choice of club, then decided to hit the ball "harder." Mistake. The harder you hit, the higher the ball will climb. And when it does that, you'll finish short of your target.

There are two things you can do. First, take at least one more club than you initially think you need to make the distance. That's obvious. Second, try to flight the ball lower than normal.

To hit lower you have to de-loft the club by turning the back of your left hand down into impact and/or reduce your swing speed. Both will produce a low-flying shot.

For a really low shot move the ball back in your stance and abbreviate your through swing. The more the club points down through the shot the more you will hit the ball down. Feel like your hands are releasing the club to a definite point of extension, pointing the club down to the ground.

9. Downwind

Sometimes a helping downwind can cause you as many problems as a strong headwind. Shots can be hard to control if you simply blast the ball skyward. With a helping breeze, who knows where they will come down?

Then again, from the tee you are generally looking for as much distance as possible. To

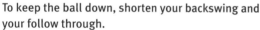
To keep the ball down, shorten your backswing and your follow through.

that end, use your 3-wood on downwind holes. The longer the ball is in the air, the longer the wind will have to carry it forward. Plus, you'll be more accurate. There is no downside.

10. Uneven lies

These are inevitable and can be unsettling if you don't follow a few simple rules.

The key is to get yourself into the address position that allows you to go ahead and make your regular swing. You always want your shoulders to be set up so that they are at about 90 degrees to the slope, just as if you are

standing on level ground. Instead of standing relative to the horizon, you are standing level to the ground you are standing on.

Be aware, though. When you change your setup, the shape of your swing will also change. For example, if the ball is above your feet, and you stand taller, your swing will automatically flatten. In turn, that will tend to make you hook the ball.

To counteract that factor, your emphasis needs to be on making a more rounded swing. Think "turn."

On the other side of the coin, when the ball is below your feet, you need to bend over more from your hips to compensate. This

On an uphill lie, set your shoulders parallel to the upslope.

On a downhill lie, try to get your shoulders parallel to the downslope.

With the ball above your feet, stand more upright.

With the ball below your feet, lean over the ball more from your hips.

time, your tendency will be to make a more upright swing and hit a cut. This time think up and down.

There are any number of slopes you'll have to play from, of course, but among the most common are the uphill and downhill lies.

If your ball stops on an up-slope, focus again on your shoulders. Set up so that they are at right angles to the slope. This will add loft to your club and, later, the shot. So take at least one club more. Be aware, also, that the ball will tend to hook because you can't turn your hips through the shot as much as you would like. Aim a touch right to allow for that.

The downhill lie is even more difficult, certainly more intimidating. But the same principles apply. Get your shoulders parallel to the slope. Aim a little left because the shot will tend to cut. And take one club less than you would normally need for the distance. The extra loft will help get the ball up.

Your swing should be a little more upright than you would normally make. Your body will want to turn through more, so you need to compensate for that in order to make solid contact.

In general, you can remove a lot of the fear from all of these shots by setting up properly and compensating for the slope with your aim. If you do both, it is a lot easier just to let things happen. Don't try to figure out where to put the ball in your stance and all that stuff. The only reason for doing that would be if you were not standing level to the ground you are on.